Karen O'Brien was born in New Zealand in 1958 and moved to London in 1981. She has worked in television – for Reuters, the BBC and CNN – and is now a producer for BBC World Service and a freelance writer. She has published one other book, *Women's Work: A Sourcebook for Women in the Workforce* and writes on women's issues and music for national newspapers and magazines.

HYMN TO HER

WOMEN MUSICIANS TALK

Karen O'Brien

Published by VIRAGO PRESS Limited April 1995
20 Vauxhall Bridge Road, London SW1V 2SA

*A CIP catalogue record for this book is available from the
British Library*

Typeset by M Rules
Printed in Great Britain by
Cox & Wyman Ltd, Reading, Berkshire

This book is dedicated, with thanks and affection,
to the women featured in it

CONTENTS

Acknowledgements

This book has been a labour of love. My thanks to the following for making that labour a little easier: Paul Charles at Asgard, Steve Coe at Moonsung, Ron Fierstein and Melissa Bailey at AGF, Amanda Freeman and Sandra MacKay at RMP, Kaja Gula at Side One, Karen Krattinger at Senior Management, Ken Levitan at Vector Management, Ilene Mark at Watt Works Inc, Mark Marnie, Gaylene Martin at Partridge and Storey, Julia Morris at Bamn Management, Michael Phillips, Steve Swallow and Deborah Thackery-Tyers.

Special thanks to Becky Swift at Virago for her encouragement and enthusiasm; to New York's finest: Kenny Kramer, Susan Noss, and Ron Maranian, to my mother, Fay, for sharing the joy of words and music, and to Tony, with my love and gratitude.

And, especially, thank you to the inspiring – and inspired – musicians who are featured in this book.

This temptation to pretend that women are non-existent musically, to ignore or damp down our poor little triumphs . . . is a microbe that will flourish comfortably, though perhaps surreptitiously, in the male organism, till there are enough women composers for it to die a natural death. Whereupon men will forget it ever existed. Have they not already forgotten their frenzied opposition to 'Votes for Women'?

ETHEL SMYTH

■

Composing a piece of music is very feminine. It is sensitive, emotional, contemplative. By comparison, doing housework is positively masculine.

BARBARA KOLB

■

The art of music is so deep and profound that to approach it very seriously is not enough. One must approach music with a serious rigour and, at the same time, with a great affectionate joy.

NADIA BOULANGER

■

I can't stand to sing the same song the same way two nights in succession. If you can, then it ain't music, it's close order drill, or exercise, or yodelling, or something, not music.

BILLIE HOLIDAY

■

I am a genius. I am not your clown. Most of you people out there are crooks. I am an artist, not an entertainer . . . and five record companies owe me money.

NINA SIMONE

Introduction

It's a cyclical thing: every now and then the music industry discovers women. The discovery often comes about as a result of the publicity-hungry marriage of convenience between record companies and music journalists, eager for the Next Big Thing – the next big talent, the next big marketing budget, the next big sales figure.

Women, of course, have always been here, making music, writing songs, performing their work. But they're often just made to sit quietly and wait their turn. Witness the '60s girl groups and folkie protest singers; the '70s sensitive singer-songwriters and the rock chicks; the punks, rappers and sensitive singer-songwriters (second generation) of the '80s; and most recently, the Angry Young Women of the '90s Riot Girl scene.

Riot Girl, an American 'discovery', emerged in the British music papers as a response to ageing male scribes posing the question, 'Can Women Rock?' Acres of trees were felled to provide sufficient paper to cover both sides of the argument. It was a debate which any self-respecting woman musician, Riot Girl or not, could have answered by saying simply, without excuses, without justifications: 'Of course we can . . . if we *want* to!'

The role of women in the music industry is constantly changing and becoming stronger as increasing numbers of women resist the market's – and often their management's – pressures to conform to the non-threatening stereotypes, the safe, saccharine images. But pick up any music publication or reference book and you'll find a world overwhelmingly dominated by men – the performers, the managers, the promoters, agents, the writers. In an insomniac moment, I counted the number of articles, however brief, about women musicians in one leading mainstream British music publication – just six, excluding the reviews (and of these only a small proportion were of work by women musicians). And in an equivalent American publication, there were seven articles, including an obituary, and again, some were little more than a few lines.

In this book, Carla Bley – who is widely acknowledged as being among the finest jazz composers of the past thirty years – shrugs off her exclusion from the American Encyclopaedia of Jazz, '. . . because the editor didn't like my music!' That omission has now been rectified, and clearly it didn't hamper Bley's career but what does it say about the ways in which music history is compiled and preserved? What message does it give aspiring composers and musicians, hungry for knowledge? How does it foster in them a sense of being part of something as universal and powerful as music? Very often, it doesn't.

Reality is, fortunately, far less limited – and limiting. I began writing about music as an antidote to the news journalism that dominates my working life. I actively sought out work by women because of my frustration at this woeful under-representation in so many publications and books, this information drought. I found a parallel universe of gifted and creative musicians, many of whom were redefining the boundaries of music. So often, the media images that do prevail are at odds with reality. It's hard to believe we are halfway through the knowledgeable New Age '90s, when the old clichés about women playing acoustic guitars, women with short hair and sensible shoes, women wearing make-up and dresses are being trotted out in the same way as they were *thirty* years ago! It's time we moved far beyond that.

Women are surrounded by the issues of image and presentation, the cultural and social pressures to conform, in a way that few men are. It's the syndrome which Sheila Chandra describes as '. . . sound pretty, be accessible and don't be dangerous'. Suzanne Vega and Tanita Tikaram both released new albums at about the same time they had their hair cut. You might think that hair cuts are something fairly innocuous and entirely unrelated to one's body of work. That is, until you read some of the reviews. Hair cut and colour loomed large in many a writer's mind. I have yet to read a review of albums by Eric Clapton or Bruce Springsteen or Guns N'Roses which highlights Eric's new haircut, or Bruce's leather jacket, or Axl Rose's leggings.

These ironies are not lost on the women themselves. As Jane Siberry says, 'The good writers come up with unusual comparisons but they really are comparing more essential qualities than whether you all have high cheekbones or you're blonde or have a crack in your voice.' Kirsty MacColl muses, '. . . like most women, I know, I would like to be thinner, but would it make my records or my job or my life any better?' And for Tanita Tikaram the frustration of misrepresentation comes when 'So many interviews are done by men who reduce women's writing, it's just belittled . . . they say, "women's writing is to do with the interior", as if that's a criticism, how can you write a song which doesn't come from inside?'

Few women have been subject to the vitriolic media criticism which has been levelled at Yoko Ono – and generally, for reasons which had nothing to do with her musical ability. With tongue in cheek, she admits that her marriage to John Lennon was not exactly a smart career move for either of them. But if there was a price to pay for falling in love with a rock icon, today Yoko Ono is philosophical: 'I didn't like the fact that I was attacked, I thought "why is this happening to me?" There were times when we were depressed . . . but together we accomplished some good things, and compared to that, and the excitement of being in love, the attacks were minuscule.'

Women in music may take themselves seriously and value their art – most do – but this is no guarantee that the industry will comply. Suzanne Vega ruefully recalls being turned down by 'every major label in America – some of them, twice!' That included the record company which eventually signed her, and for which she has sold millions of records. Janis Ian was fourteen years old when her song, 'Society's Child' was turned down by twenty-two record companies because at the time – the early '60s – its theme of an inter-racial love affair was considered to be commercial suicide. One company eventually took a chance and the song brought Janis Ian international success, and became known as one of the classics of socially-conscious writing.

Janis Ian took another commercial risk when, in 1993, she made it known publicly that she was a lesbian: 'I know here and there which record companies turned me down because they did not want another lesbian on their label: to quote one, "we've got enough lesbians already!" '

And of the commercial pressures which few musicians – women and men – escape, Rosanne Cash says, 'If I sell a million records, that's success according to the record company; but if I sell one hundred and fifty thousand, that's a failure. If one hundred and fifty thousand people are really moved, doesn't that mean *something*?'

The desire to create music beyond the realm of the formulaic mainstream, 'baby, I love you so much!' ersatz emotions is something all of these musicians share. Moe Tucker says, 'I'd feel stupid singing, "oh baby, don't go, I'll die if you leave me" because I'm not thinking that; if I'm going to write a song, I can't think of what to say unless it means something to me.' These musicians hold a mirror up and reflect, in words and music, much of what they see in a troubled world. Suzanne Vega's vignette of an abused child, 'Luka', was one of the most unlikely commercial successes of the 1980s, tackling an issue that had rarely been questioned musically, and certainly not in the pop charts. It was a theme echoed by Janis Ian on the haunting 'Breaking Silence', and on 'His Hands', which had its roots in her own painful marriage to a violent man. The same experience led Nanci Griffith to write songs like 'Fragile' and 'Ford Econoline'; she says she writes of abuse, 'not in a bitter way but in a way of overcoming it . . . they're not protest songs, they're healing songs'. These are women for whom it's simply not enough to survive, we must be able to *thrive* as well.

Neneh Cherry was a mother in her teens, and Monie Love when barely into her twenties, and in their music, both have celebrated motherhood *and* safe, responsible sex. And both are wary of being seen too literally as role models. As Cherry says, 'If I want to give anything to young women and young men . . . it's to inspire that person to have self-confidence and get some sort of inner strength or positivity . . . but you can't do things in a way that another person has done them.' In her song, 'Born 2 BREED', Monie Love urges people to 'Build Relationships where Education and Enlightenment Dominate'. And, she says, 'If I'm your role model, then I suggest you make your own decisions, and follow your own mind and your own trials and errors . . . be your own woman.'

Diverse as these women are, there are central themes running through these interviews, connecting them to each other in a way that is not simply defined by their gender but has more to do with individual character. There is a determination and a belief in oneself that is inspiring. As Kirsty MacColl says, 'It's what separates the women from the girlies!'

Evelyn Glennie had already begun to learn music as a child, when it became increasingly clear that her hearing was deteriorating so badly that it would soon be non-existent. Yet for her, there was no question of allowing that latent musical talent to remain untapped: 'As a child, if you fall off your bike, you get on it again and start riding . . . it's the same when you lose a faculty, then everything else compensates . . . the word "problem" doesn't arise; it only comes from other people's lips.' Nanci Griffith struggled to make sense of the written word, as a child, until it was discovered that she was dyslexic; she went on to teach young children, and later writing became the cornerstone of her musical work.

It had never occurred to Carla Bley that she didn't 'qualify' as a jazz musician when, at seventeen, she stood selling cigarettes in New York's famous jazz club, Birdland, immersed in the music of Miles Davis, Anita O'Day and John Coltrane: 'I never asked anybody how to belong, or if I could belong . . I was just very sure of what I was doing.'

Yoko Ono recalls her father's strong encouragement to become a concert pianist, in fulfilment of his own frustrated ambition to devote himself to music, but when she told him she wanted to become a composer: 'He said, there are not many women composers in the world, maybe it's a question of women's aptitude, women may not be good creators of music but they're good at interpreting music.' Her three decades in avant-garde and rock music shows that the theory of gender aptitude may be less than relevant.

Angelique Kidjo knew she would have to leave Benin to be free to create the kind of music she wanted to: 'I could either stay in Benin and use my music to praise the revolution, or I could leave. A lot of girl singers in Africa are fighting against society, they're fighting against the government.'

What has been heartening in these interviews is the way in which these musicians have paid tribute to other women, as sources of strength and encouragement, as inspiration. It's a rare man who ever acknowledges that his music has been influenced by the work of a woman, even when it so clearly has. And, to my surprise, two very well-known women musicians refused to be featured in this book, because it was about women. It's sad to think there are still women who feel that a thing has no value unless it involves men.

But the women in this book are much more generous. As Nanci Griffith says, 'If you're secure in who you are and what you are then you can shine the flashlight on someone else . . . and say, "look at this!"' and Suzanne Vega is encouraged by the number of women in music today, 'It's good that you have so many different women coming up now . . . each one is able to stand in her own light and be admired for her individual strengths.'

In this book, I wanted to show the great diversity of what women are creating in music today – whether it's classical or rap, pop or avant-garde, rock or hip hop, folk or jazz. How they shape, in dynamic or subtle forms, the music we hear every day – at home, on the radio, on television, in films. And how they are capable of so much more than the narrow strictures to which so many women musicians have been confined. I hope it has gone some way to doing that.

There was also a feeling of wanting to celebrate women's achievements, to celebrate the values and the strengths which they bring to the world of music, in all its forms, and without which that world would be much poorer. To quote Jane Siberry, 'It's important that all the resonance we feel when we speak to women is there for a reason . . . it's a gift, it's a sensitivity, that's going to be necessary to turn things around. And anything that strengthens that, like what you're doing with this book, when you see that, you have to say, yes, yes, yes, you have my total support!'

Karen O'Brien
London, 1994

Yoko Ono

Yoko Ono was born in Tokyo, Japan, in 1933. She was sent to a school for musically gifted children, and studied classical piano, encouraged to learn about western classical music by her father, and about traditional Japanese vocal forms by her mother. She took lessons in German *Lieder* and went on to university, studying philosophy and writing poetry. In 1953, she moved to the United States with her family, where she resumed her university studies at Sarah Lawrence in Bronxville, New York, and continued her writing. The works of avant-garde musicians like Edgar Varèse, Harry Coles, Arnold Schoenberg and John Cage, echoed her own musical experimentation, and here she found her *métier*. She married music student Toshi Ichiyanagi, and they moved to New York City where, by the early '60s, Yoko Ono had become part of the eclectic group of artists known as Fluxus — they were devoted to demolishing the boundaries between art and life with their 'happenings', combining music, visual art, poetry and drama. She published a book of 'instructional poems', *Grapefruit*, and became involved in experimental film-making. She first performed as a solo artist in Japan in 1962; the same year, she divorced Ichiyanagi and married Anthony Cox. Their daughter, Kyoko, was born the following year.

In 1966, she held a solo exhibition of her work at London's Indica Gallery, where she met John Lennon for the first time. She continued her musical performances, which included a concert at the Royal Albert Hall, with Ornette

Coleman, and appearances at universities. Yoko Ono was making films, producing *Bottoms* in 1967, which was initially refused a certificate by the British Board of Film Classification which deemed the subject matter – more than three hundred naked human bottoms – as unsuitable for public exhibition. In 1968, she made *Rape*, in which a woman is followed continuously by a camera-crew – at first she welcomes the attention, then becomes increasingly agitated at the relentless and horribly intrusive nature of that attention. In the same year, she began an artistic and personal partnership with John Lennon which was to last for the next twelve years, accompanied by a seemingly relentless stream of anti-Yoko criticism by many Beatles fans and sections of the media. The couple recorded 'Unfinished Music No. 1: Two Virgins' which was released on The Beatles' Apple label. If the collaboration startled music-buyers used to associating Lennon with The Beatles exclusively, the cover, which featured the couple in the nude, proved even more controversial.

Yoko Ono and John Lennon launched their campaign of protests, performances and appearances to draw attention to social issues and their call for world peace – after their marriage in 1969, they staged their celebrated 'Bed-In' protest at an Amsterdam hotel. Two months later, at a 'Bed-In' protest in Montreal, they recorded their first single, 'Give Peace a Chance', which gave the newly christened Plastic Ono Band a Top Ten hit in Britain, and reached the Top Twenty in the US. The two other album releases of that year were 'Unfinished Music No 2: Life with the Lions' and 'The Wedding Album'. In 1970, a live recording of the Plastic Ono Band's appearance at a Toronto concert hinted at the work that was to appear soon after on Yoko Ono's first solo album, 'Yoko Ono/Plastic Ono Band'. The following year she released the double-album, 'Fly', which included the soundtrack to her short film of the same name (which previewed on US television in 1972). Years later, both works were acknowledged to have been precursors of the punk and New Wave music and spoken-word artists which were to follow them.

Feminism had become a major part of Yoko Ono's life and it became an integral theme in her music – beginning with 'Sisters, O Sisters' in 1971, and dominating the albums 'Approximately Infinite Universe' (1972) and 'Feeling the Space'. Through her, Lennon, too, embraced feminism and they co-wrote 'Woman is the Nigger of the World', which was to become an international slogan for the feminist movement.

The early 1970s brought public and personal turmoil – a bitter custody dispute over, and separation from, her daughter, Kyoko; miscarriages; a lengthy battle with US Immigration authorities; drug problems and separation from Lennon. By late 1975, all of this seemed behind them – and the birth of Sean in October of that year led to a five-year 'retirement'. In late-1980 Yoko Ono and John Lennon emerged to critical and commercial acclaim with their 'Double Fantasy' album, which later received a Grammy award. On December 8, as the couple were about to enter their apartment building, John Lennon was shot dead by Mark Chapman. The mourning, loss, anger and eventual recovery that Yoko Ono experienced was chronicled on her 1981 album, 'Season of Glass' – which drew harsh criticism for the cover, which showed Lennon's bloodstained glasses – and on 'It's Alright' (1983) and 'Starpeace' (1986). In exploring issues of violent loss, her 1993 sculpture exhibition, 'Family Album: Blood Objects' became controversial, after claims – although untrue – that she was selling bronze casts of the bullet-riddled, bloodstained shirt in which John Lennon died.

A retrospective exhibition of her conceptual art at New York's Whitney Museum in 1989 marked a revival of interest in her visual work and led to other exhibitions around the world. In 1992, Rykodisc released a six-CD anthology spanning her recording career, leading to a reappraisal of her music, its influences on contemporary artists and its belated accessibility. In April 1994, Yoko Ono premiered her rock musical 'New York Rock' at the WPA Theatre in New York City – it used more than thirty of her songs to chronicle a painful but ultimately uplifting story of love, loss and renewal amid the violence of modern urban life. Critics drew strong parallels between the story and events in her life.

Yoko Ono lives in New York City.

My father was very encouraging, but it was to realise his dream, because he gave up being a pianist. His father wanted him to become a banker but before that, he had given concerts; he was a very good pianist. So he wanted his first child, regardless of whether it was a daughter or a son, to become a pianist. So, at four years old, I was sent to a school which taught children perfect pitch and harmony, how to write scores and piano technique. In teaching music very early on like that, it was a very liberal school. Several famous Japanese composers went there. Going to that school was a very important experience for me, it helped me a lot all through my life.

My parents put me in the school because they wanted me to have a good musical training, with the idea of becoming a pianist but of course that didn't go very far. I think that was because my father was really too determined about it. I remember how he would spread my fingers to see how far they would go across the keys. If I played a musical piece, I had to finish it, not just play part of it. I was never allowed to just play around. When I was born, my father was in San Francisco. When I was two and a half years old, my mother and I joined him there. The first thing he did when he saw me was pull my fingers. At that point, my fingers went into shock! I remember that very well.

We went back and forth between America and Japan. It was the '30s and there was a lot of prejudice against orientals. Because we were upper middle class, there was less suffering obviously, but we still avoided any conflict. My mother was always very careful; when she cooked with soy sauce, she would close the window, so the smell of the soy sauce wouldn't get out. I remember, although the war had not yet started, there was a lot of oriental-bashing. When I'd go to see films, the baddie was always oriental and people in the cinema would be booing. It was embarrassing because the lights would go on at the end and I'd think, 'Do they think I'm bad, too?'

I think it's important to note in the making of what I am now, those times where my mother was always telling me to be careful about not making a bad impression. She didn't want the neighbours to complain about us. My mother used to say to me, if I was a bad girl, 'People will not say that Yoko is a bad girl, they will say that all orientals are bad.' I took that in. It was a burden for a child. I felt I had the responsibility for myself, and representing my country, and also living out my father's wish of being a concert pianist, when I really wasn't capable of that. It was a strain.

I remember being six or seven years old, just a young child, walking along the street and other children would throw stones at me. It was frightening, the tension was already there. I actually *felt* the tension. We were advised to leave and go back to Japan and that year, the war started. Back in Japan, I felt caught in the middle, between Japan and America, where I had lived and where I had friends. I was in a precarious position because in those days, when somebody came back to Japan from America, who had obviously picked up American ways, people would often throw stones at them. They didn't throw stones at me but I remember thinking it was harsh. I have felt, so often in my life, that I was always in the position of being a bridge between two separate things, of always trying to see both sides.

By the time I was fourteen or fifteen, I really felt that I wanted to be a composer and a poet. I realised that those two things were my forte. As a child, I was always writing poetry and although I was taking piano lessons, I secretly preferred the side of me that was the writer. My father was startled that I wanted to go that way. He was very good about it but at the time, he was concerned for me because he had observed, from history, there had been no great women composers. So, he thought that maybe women were not particularly good at composing;

perhaps women didn't have the capability, or the aptitude – although there were many good women pianists, who interpreted other people's music. He didn't have the usual prejudices against women, as in 'women shouldn't do this or that'; it wasn't that, it was just what he had innocently observed from history. Well, firstly we don't know if there were no great women composers; we just may not be told about them! And there have always been so many pressures on them. There were many great women writers but few women composers, and that has to do with the fact that writing is an acceptable art form for a woman. In order to compose, maybe you have to play the piano, you have to make a noise but in writing, you can do it quietly, you can do it early in the morning when the children are asleep, or at the kitchen table – writing was done that way by women.

If you compose, you don't necessarily have to make a lot of noise, you can do it by writing, by hearing the music in your head, but at some point, the music has to be played by someone, it has to be performed. Then, you're working with other musicians and how many musicians back then wanted to play music composed by women?

My father said, 'You write poetry and you like writing and you do that well. Maybe what you want to be is a singer. That way, you can satisfy your need to keep in touch with poetry and music' – not that I would write the songs but that I would sing other people's!

When I was young, and trying to write music, I realised that rather than write scores laboriously it was easier to express the music in lines, in straight lines, zigzag lines. It was a way of showing more precisely what I wanted the musicians to do. That may have something to do with the fact that in oriental music, there is no western kind of notation; there is a different way of expressing the sound. The fact that the notation had to be exactly like western music was not fixed in my mind. I had this tradition of another form of notation and that opened up my mind.

I noticed when I got up early, there was an incredible sound of birds singing in the garden. In my music school, the kind of exercise they'd make us do would be to take any noise we heard on a daily basis – birds or trains or whatever – and translate the noise of daily life on to paper. For instance, if you heard the telephone ringing, you'd say, 'what is that note?' So always, when you were walking or playing or whatever, you'd be thinking of that noise, that note. You trained yourself to translate the noises into notations. It was a very important exercise. I was listening to the birds and I thought, 'I can't notate this because the birdsong, and its beat, is just so complex'. I thought it would be so great if I *could* notate it and create music out of it. I thought there must be a way of just putting that birdsong into a song and to then translate that into a notation.

At Sarah Lawrence, I was describing this to my composition teacher, saying, 'There are some sounds you just can't translate into notations.' Then he told me there were people who were trying to create that kind of music – the avant-garde musicians like Edgar Varèse, who were living in New York City. So I was writing, trying to combine birdsong with the flute or other instruments. Then, when I went to New York, by chance I met John Cage and his group of artists, such as Christian Wolfe and Morton Feldman. Then there was the younger generation, like Richard Maxfield and LaMonte Young, people who were later called the Fluxus group. I felt immediately that I belonged to that group; we had similar sensibilities and we inspired each other.

I was in love with all different forms of art and that was probably the difference between me and the others. The men tended to label themselves as 'sculptor' or 'painter', and it became their career. But, as a woman, I felt I could be free of the usual route. Most women are outsiders; I was an outsider, as a woman among those men. All of us are, in the sense that we live in a society dominated by men. Men are encouraged to be tough, from a very young age; they're told to choose a career and become a person who is defined by that. Women, primarily, are ignored.

In those days, people didn't say to a woman, 'What do you do?' Women were either beautiful or not very beautiful; they were either married or unmarried. In a way, if you wanted to be somebody, there was no encouragement, no focusing on what you were going to be. But while most of my friends, the avant-garde artists, were either painters or composers, I felt free to jump from one medium to another, to express whatever I was feeling.

In the New York avant-garde scene that I was in, there was definitely a feeling of 'Why is this woman doing something?' There was a certain kind of grouping where all of the guys did group concerts, but I was never included. When I did a series of influential concerts with LaMonte Young, there was a story going around that they were LaMonte's concerts and he was just using my loft. There was another odd story, when people heard the concerts were with someone called Young, that 'Yoko has a very rich Chinese patron who is making her do this!' LaMonte Young was white and American; it was just because of the name!

So, I just did my own thing; I did solo concerts. Not being invited into a group allowed me to do my own work, in my own way. Interestingly, my name became more prominent than theirs in a way, because they were seen as part of a group whereas I was seen as a solo artist. Even now, women musicians still get flak and are still in a more difficult position than male musicians. I want them to know that if they're doing their own thing, there is *always* a way. The conventional way may not be open to us as much, because it is set up for men. If the door closes, don't worry about it; maybe you don't need that door to be open. For women musicians who think that the doors don't open as quickly as they do for men, as long as you don't limit yourself, then the right doors will always open. The important thing is to recognise the right door when it is open to you. Sometimes we keep knocking at the wrong door for ages, though that is a lesson as well. So you don't have to regret it.

In hindsight there is always a blessing. Even in the limitations that are put on us. I think that it was a blessing that my father was so eager for me to be a pianist; it led me to my musical interests. I didn't become what he wanted me to become; it made me *not* become a pianist. And the fact that my mother was such an incredible artist made me more conceptual in my visual art because I knew I could never draw like her. So, everything is a blessing.

I was never really interested in becoming a visual artist. I was always interested in becoming a composer or a writer. The reason for this was very similar to the reason I never wanted to be a pianist: I was the daughter of two frustrated artists. Just as my father was a great pianist, my mother was an incredible painter. My uncle was a painter and another uncle was a sculptor. My mother was probably better than both of them but she gave it up to be a wife and mother. But that frustration was always there in her and she was always sketching. When I was a little girl, and I had to do some drawings as my homework for school, my mother would come in and say, 'Let me show you, you've got the balance wrong; let me just do it for you.' I remember once, I took this beautiful drawing to school, which she'd done, and the teacher said, 'This can't be yours, it's too good!' I was so embarrassed, it was not what I'd wanted to do, it just ended up with my mother correcting everything. I always felt I could never be like my mother. But I was always a lover of visual art and for that, I have to give credit to my mother. From an early age, I was taught how to look at a painting, how to look at the lines, the colour and the balance.

———————————— ■ ————————————

I consider 1966 a magical year for me. By then, I was very active in doing gallery shows, and as a composer in New York. I was a very New York type of person, I considered it the centre of the world! I didn't feel the need to go anywhere else. But in 1966, I was invited to Connecticut, an hour away from New York, to do a show at the Wesleyan University. It went very well; it was a very inspiring two or three days. It was then that I realised that

I could communicate with people outside New York! It was opportunities like that, which came from outside like magic, that opened my eyes to the outside world. My life has been full of coincidences, the most important moves have been things that just happened and I went with the flow, rather than what I had intended to do. If you're open to the future, things *will* come to you. And what comes into your future that way can be more beautiful than anything you'd planned.

Then, I was invited back to England to take part in the 'Destruction of Art' symposium and after that, one thing led to another. People who saw my work at the symposium invited me to do a solo show at the Indica Gallery in London. From John's point of view, that was the first time he'd heard of me. He came to see the show and we met. There was a kind of fleeting flash in me at that moment. To me, he appeared to be beautiful. But I was married, I had a child, I was the bread-winner. All that responsibility was heavy on my shoulders. Also I was serious about my work as an artist and my time was devoted to being that. But just for a fleeting moment, I wished I didn't have all those responsibilities. That feeling lasted about two seconds! And then, he just suddenly grabbed the apple [part of her display of conceptual art] and took a bite out of it, and that just turned me off! I thought, 'Oh, dear, I'm sorry I thought that!' It was just a fleeting moment of 'I wish' followed by 'oh, no!' It took until May 1968 for us to get together.

The *Bottoms* film also came about as a coincidence. A man said he would put up the money if I made a feature-length film. I already had a film of bottoms that I had made in New York; it was only two or three minutes long. But this had to be a feature film. So I said, 'I have an idea. How about an hour-long film of bottoms?' The man said, 'OK!' I like to have a real tongue-in-cheek quality to my work so instead of coming up with some deep and complex filmic idea, I thought it would be hilarious that I would do a feature-length film of the three-minute version. First of all, it's a dumb idea to just have bottoms for three minutes, now, it's humongously dumb to have three hundred and sixty-five bottoms in a feature film! I liked that. I went ahead and made the film since this guy promised me he would put up the money – but he didn't.

When the British Board of Film Classification banned it, it became news. It was on television, and the TV report showed the bottoms! It was great – only in England, I thought! I was very proud of the British for that. Part of me was not very happy that the film was successful because I felt that I'd made so many creative and original things, when suddenly here was a film that I'd made as a throwaway, 'let's just have fun' kind of thing. All the other pieces had been much more serious and intellectual and complex than this piece, and they didn't get the attention that the *Bottoms* film got.

The *Bottoms* film was so successful that much later I found out that people behind the Iron Curtain had heard of it. I don't know how. It was the *only* thing they knew of me! Fate had taken me to this point of 'success' which was totally inadvertent. And all my artistic friends started to drop me; their excuse was that I had become vulgar and commercial, 'She sold out so we're not inviting her to dinner any more!' So I was caught up in the air and feeling very lonely.

John had built up his image and career in a certain way and people accepted that. I, in my own way, had built up my career which was accepted by my world. So people were used to labelling him and me in a certain way. Then, when we got together, it was very confusing for people. The avant-garde world spoke of me as if I'd died: 'That's the end of Yoko's career!' And of course, in the rock world, people saw it as the end of John's career. So, in that sense it was not a very good move for either of us. But we weren't saying, 'Oh, this is a disastrous career move, but regardless of that we're getting together.' We were too busy being in love and never thought of it from that angle.

Of course I didn't like the fact that I was attacked; I was

thinking why is this happening? When I got together with John, I realised that the amount of press attention I'd been getting up till then could not compare with this. I really didn't know it would be like that, that wherever we went it would be in the papers. So I thought it was important to use that media, instead of being used *by* it; to do something with it and make a statement about world peace. So we conjured up the Bed-In idea and did it. The Bed-In was the combination of John's daring and my daring; together we were almost impossible, I suppose! It was almost like 'we made our bed' but we didn't know it at the time. Our priority was our work and through our work, to change the world. Again, what was interesting was the fact that fate almost put me in a situation where I'm bridging western culture and eastern culture and the avant-garde and rock worlds.

We accomplished some good things together and compared to the excitement of falling in love, inspiring each other and learning about a world that we had never encountered before, the pain of being attacked was a minuscule matter; it was more like an education. We were very thankful for what we had together, working together, having the family.

What we're doing as artists is just information and inspiration for others. The thing is, if they don't get any information because they don't choose to see it or hear it, it's their own loss. It's not our loss, because we experienced the pleasure of making it. When a journalist writes something because of his or her need to make money, or please their ego, and becomes a wall to block the information rather than being a bridge, it becomes a loss to the people.

———————————————■———————————————

I had already had the idea for the *Rape* film by the time John and I got together, so I was not aware of the parallel situation I would be in, in my own life, of the parallel intrusions. So after John's passing, when I saw *Rape* I couldn't believe it; I got chills. But there are a lot of situations like that. John went through the same thing with 'Lucy in the Sky with Diamonds'; some people considered it was about LSD and he just didn't realise.

I only create when I'm inspired, and sometimes I don't really know what I'm making or the true reason I'm making it. When I made 'Death of Samantha', I wasn't at all aware of what was going to happen. When John passed away, the fans all sent me 'Death of Samantha' verses and said, 'you were talking about the vigil' and I read it and it registered with me. Because it was my death too, part of me died with John. I couldn't believe that I wrote this song, never knowing that it would be a flash of the future.

The albums I made since John's death – 'Season of Glass', 'It's Alright' and 'Starpeace' – were made at a time when I was in sheer pain. Just the act of going into the studio and concentrating my mind on work and the music was very healing. It was very important for me because otherwise I would have gone crazy; somehow music kept me from becoming totally insane.

The cover of 'Season of Glass', I felt, was a way to communicate what had happened to John; I wanted people to know that. It was a very small part of what had happened. I saw much more blood than that; it was a very mild way of showing people what a violent act it had been. I was surprised when I got a phone call from Geffen Records, saying that the record stores would not stock the record unless I changed the cover. My feeling was that people would understand. And I refused to change the cover.

Also with the 'Blood Objects', I thought that was a very normal thing to do, to show family violence. And showing that men are victims of violence too. It was taken wrongly by some people because of the way the media falsely described it. Of course the press have to always write something sensational; to write 'it was a good exhibition' is not news, so they resort to creative journalism! The media takes us further and further from reality and the truth suffers for it.

I'm a feminist but at the same time it's very important that we understand the male point of view as well, because we are together and half of the world is men. It's almost as though we are in the same boat but we don't know where we're going. Is there going to be an apocalypse or are we going to survive together as a human race? It makes sense to work together. You can only do that if you are very independent. It seems like a dichotomy but unless you are independent, you can't come together. We're not independent when we're blaming the men for all the difficulties. We have to take responsibility as well.

If you look for difficulties, I'm sure there's a lot of them. But it's in the way you look at it, too. The fact that all the doors were closed to me, and I suffered attacks on an international level, was very good for me. In hindsight, that really helped me to be strong. It made me wise, and no matter how many doors were closed to me, the real doors kept opening.

It's important to be open to everything that comes to you. Instead of saying, 'this is not my plan, I'm going to reject this', it's important to be open, to go with the flow, instead of being obstinate about your initial plan. What comes to you might be bigger and more beautiful. I made the *Bottoms* film from nothing; the money wasn't given, after all, but it was achieved through the work; it wasn't the money that did it. Anybody who's sitting there thinking, 'I can't do this because I don't have the money', or 'I can't do it because of this or that', think about other ways of doing it.

When John passed away and I had this big lump in my stomach, I didn't know what to do about it. Then I realised that this sorrow could eat me up, this sorrow and anger could make me sick. It was very difficult to do, but the only way I was able to do it was to focus my mind on something else. So, I told myself to do three good things a day; whatever the three good things are, it could be tiny, it could be big. I focus on that rather than the difficulties.

We have to be wise to survive. Instead of allowing the

sorrow and anger and resentment to build this wall around us, we have to focus on doing something positive. Even if you can only do something good for your family or for your neighbour, then do that. That's the connection. Keep doing your work; work is a sanctuary, and it doesn't have to be some grandiose, noble, brilliant work. It could just be calling your neighbour and saying 'how are you doing', but to care for something other than yourself. Keep on doing that and the walls you've built up will disappear; that's what I did to survive.

Suzanne Vega

S uzanne Vega was born in Santa Monica, California in
1959. She grew up in a Hispanic neighbourhood in New
York City, believing she was half-Puerto Rican, until her novel-
ist father told her that he was really her step-father, and that her
biological father was white and had not seen her since she was a
baby. This sparked something of an identity crisis, which eventually culminated in a reunion with her biological father almost
twenty years later. She later discovered that her paternal grandmother had also been a musician, a drummer with the Merry
Makers' Ladies Orchestra in the US in the 1920s and '30s.

As a teenager, Suzanne Vega attended the High School of
the Performing Arts (immortalised in the film/television series,
'Fame'), where she studied dance. Teaching herself to play the
guitar, she began to write songs, fuelled by discovering the
music of Leonard Cohen and Lou Reed. By the time she
attended her first rock concert – a Lou Reed show – at the age
of nineteen, she had abandoned her plans to become a dancer
and, while at Barnard College, performed her own songs in student cafés and the folk clubs of Greenwich Village.

After leaving Barnard, she worked as a receptionist while
gradually building up a strong following for her solo acoustic
performances on the folk circuit. After numerous abortive
attempts to interest several major record companies in her demo
tape, glowing reviews from music critics wooed A & M Records
into offering her a recording contract – despite having turned
her down twice before. In April 1985, her debut album,
'Suzanne Vega', was released, produced by Lenny Kaye and her

co-manager, Steve Addabbo. Its collection of self-penned literate and understated songs, showing only a passing resemblance to neo-folk, received universal critical acclaim and Suzanne Vega came to be regarded as the vanguard of a new generation of female singer-songwriters. The album reached number eleven on the UK album chart and provided her first major singles hit, 'Marlene on the Wall'.

The following year, while continuing to tour to promote the album, she performed at a benefit concert in London for the Prince's Trust charity and featured on two recordings – the soundtrack of the John Hughes' film, *Pretty in Pink*, with her song, 'Left of Centre', and on the Smithereens' 'Especially for You' album, co-writing and singing on the track, 'A Lonely Place'. In 1987, while writing songs for her second album, she contributed two compositions to the Philip Glass album, 'Songs of Liquid Days'.

The release of her follow-up, 'Solitude Standing', was buoyed by the huge success of the single, 'Luka', which broke new ground in the pop charts, written, as it was, from the viewpoint of a child abuse victim. The song was to bring her numerous awards from organisations fighting child abuse, for the recognition it brought to the issue. It also garnered a Grammy nomination, and an MTV award for the best female video. The album reached the US Top Twenty and the UK Top Ten. Continuing her film soundtrack work, Suzanne Vega wrote the title song for the Disney compilation, *Stay Awake*.

In 1990, 'Days of Open Hand', co-produced by Suzanne Vega and Anton Sanko, was released to a mixed critical reception – while more experimental musically, it moved the focus away from the introspective viewpoint of the two previous albums, to observations of the external world. Veteran music film-maker D.A. Pennebaker shot a documentary of the preparations for, and the early part of the 'Open Hand' tour, which was shown on British and American television soon after the album was released. Later that year, a surprise money-spinner surfaced when a little-known British dance re-mix duo, DNA, released a bootleg recording of 'Tom's Diner', the a cappella track from 'Solitude Standing', with a heavy dance beat overlaid. Putting aside the option of legal action, A & M decided to release the track with Suzanne Vega's blessing. The song stayed on the British pop and dance charts for weeks.

The following year, Suzanne Vega compiled 'Tom's Album', a quirky collection of unsolicited versions of 'Tom's Diner' which she'd been sent by fans and musicians, in the wake of DNA's experimentation. She also contributed two tracks to 'Deadicated', an album of covers of Grateful Dead songs, and began writing for her new album, '99.9F', which was released in mid-1992. Produced by Mitchell Froom, it was more technically innovative than her earlier work, relying heavily on percussion, distortion and more accessible pop and techno beats. Her concert appearances included the Woody Guthrie Tribute in New York and a benefit for Italy's Berloni Foundation, organised by Luciano Pavarotti, in Modena, in aid of leukaemia patients. She toured for much of 1993 in support of '99.9F' and appeared at a benefit concert for Amnesty International in London. She has campaigned in support of Amnesty's Working Group for Children.

Suzanne Vega lives in New York City.

------------------------------- ■ -------------------------------

I'd wanted to be a performer, from the time I was five or six. I was always dancing up and down the hallway or making costumes for myself, or getting the other kids to do stuff with me, or singing to them. I had sung at Carnegie Hall when I was twelve, because of Pete Seeger. He had come to my school and picked me out, me and my sister, [to be] among a bunch of kids to sit at his feet at Carnegie Hall. That was probably my first gig.

By that point I had already decided that I wanted to be one of these famous people. I think I decided that when I was five or six. I wanted to get my name in the newspaper. Most kids feel disregarded, and what you're after is for someone to really listen to you. So you start imagining that if you're a very famous model, or the first woman on the moon, that you'll get that feeling of importance. I took myself very seriously; I knew that I was smart because everyone always said so. And I remember people thinking I was kind of amusing because I seemed so much older than I actually was, and I seemed very precocious. People thought, 'Oh, she's really cute, look at her reading there.' I didn't have any sense of what I looked like, or if I was pretty or if I was good or if I was useful. It was more important to be smart than to be sexy; some girls get attention through being sexy, whereas, although I was always interested in sex, I never felt that I needed to be sexy to get attention. I preferred doing it in a smart way.

I remember feeling very odd and very much like a target because I was easily the whitest kid [at school]. These very dark black girls would come up and touch my face and my hair because they'd never seen anybody so white especially up close like that, so I had this sense of being kind of weird and not knowing how to fit in. I was later transferred to a gifted children's class which was really racially mixed and I was really happy there because I found I could talk to the other kids. In high school, I was part of a Puerto Rican singing troupe and we would go around and sing in different boroughs; it was a government-sponsored programme to bring the Puerto Rican culture back to the Hispanic community. So we would sing these songs in Spanish and everyone there was either Puerto Rican or Cuban or Dominican and again it was always like, 'What's she doing here?' Once they heard me speak Spanish it was kind of OK but in the end, I definitely felt that I was trying to jam myself into a place that I didn't really fit into.

I grew up feeling like the odd one out even though I was told that I was actually Puerto Rican and I could speak Spanish and I had gone to Puerto Rico and I felt very comfortable with my step-father's family. He asked me one day if I'd ever wondered why I didn't look like him, and actually we look as far different as people can possibly look. So, obviously it was a big surprise [that he was not my real father] but I think it also confirmed that weird feeling of feeling different. I didn't even really click right away; mostly I just remember feeling annoyed and feeling embarrassed at being singled out, and wondering whether it was a joke of some kind. After that it was just as if it had never really happened, except occasionally one of my brothers would suddenly burst out at the dinner table and say, 'Isn't it true that Suzie has another father' and we'd all tell him to shut up!

I studied dance from the time I was nine to when I was about eighteen. I especially wanted to study the Martha Graham technique which is what I specialised in when I went to the High School of Performing Arts in 1976. [Back then] everyone wanted to be Liza Minnelli or David Bowie and everyone was dying their hair red and it was very flash. One of the first days I got there someone gave me a big hug and kissed me on both cheeks and then realised they had mistaken me for somebody else! I was very serious and tended to dress in these big sweaters and baggy clothes. Most of my friends were in the classical music department and they were considered sort of nerdy. That's where I gravitated.

I was terribly competitive, I couldn't bear to have anything less than the highest marks. But I was terribly depressed also and I found it really hard to control my body. So I was getting low marks because I was depressed and I had no energy. This really got to me because again, I felt that sense of trying to jam myself into a situation where I wasn't going to shine and where I wasn't really going to be myself or be appreciated for what I thought I was. It was a very frustrating period. Now I realise that I had certain health problems that were preventing me. I had asthma, I was anaemic, I had all these other things that I didn't know about. So I was kind of fighting the tide.

I had already started writing songs by that point and I'd started to perform them when I was about sixteen. I'd go to these different coffee-houses and I'd play the songs that I'd written. I felt very hostile towards the audience, often. I didn't get any jobs for a long time because of it! Patti Smith was the big rage, and David Bowie, so I was very, very out of fashion. Most people said to me, 'Well, you're talented and if it was ten years ago, you'd probably be a big star but you should probably just forget about it because you've got an attitude and obviously, you don't have any experience, you can't just get up on stage and sing and expect people to just come to you.'

So I would go down to these clubs in the [Greenwich] Village. There was one club where I had heard it all began, the Bitter End. This is where I understood, if you played at the Bitter End and if you got accepted there, then you could go on to Folk City and then after that you could go on to the Bottom Line. So I had this hierarchy planted very firmly in my mind. So I tried to get a gig at the Bitter End for two years – I kept getting rejected! There was one man there who would sit and eat his dinner while you were [auditioning] and he'd be sitting there drinking and eating pork chops and looking around the room. He knew me already because I'd come down every other month and I'd get rejected and leave. And then come down again.

It made me fed up but on the other hand, I had this very slow and steady stubborn way of doing things and if one person, or two people, said, 'I really like your lyrics or I really listen to you', that was enough to keep me going. I started to be method-ical about it, and keep a notebook of what songs I had sung and how I'd done my hair, and who was there, and what they said, and if I'd made any money. I was trying to control the conditions and approach it as a professional. As a dancer, for example, you know that you have to warm up, you can't just come out on stage, you have to know your cues and know the lighting. So I was approaching it the way a dancer would.

I had a very strong sense of what it was I wanted to say and I got enough encouragement so that I didn't feel I needed to change too drastically. I had no desire to get into a pop band, I hated most of the things that were fashionable. I was never really eager. I was never, 'Oh, please, sign me'. I was always like, 'Go to hell!' and if people stuck around then I figured that they were serious.

Finally, I completed a demo tape which was unanimously rejected by every major label in America, including A & M, which rejected it twice. The turning-point came when I kept getting really good reviews. A & M eventually funded a new demo and we had a production deal. The first album ['Suzanne Vega'] came out and they were expecting to sell thirty thousand copies worldwide and it sold much more than that. I had mixed feelings because on the one hand, I wasn't naïve. I was young but I wasn't naïve. I had seen people who were doing so well just go streaking through the folk scene in New York getting tremendous amounts of press and hype and then they kind of crashed. So I was aware that the record could have easily ended up in the ninety-nine cent bin.

When the album came out, I felt plucked out of the scene that I had been happily sloshing around in, plucked out and thrown around the world as an example. The thing that puzzled me was that a lot of people said, 'Oh, look, it's a folk revival, look, she's playing acoustic guitar.' And I thought, 'Wait a second, that's not what I'm really about.' Because even in the folk scene I wasn't known as being a good representation of folk music. It was more like, 'She's doing something odd, something different, she's taken the acoustic guitar and made a weird thing out of it.' But none of that seemed to be picked up by the press, all they talked about was the folk revival and it suddenly seemed like it was going to be 1964 again. That was disappointing to me because I didn't want to be a symbol of the folk revival, I wanted people to pick out what was distinctive about what I was doing.

At that point, I didn't feel connected to anything. I felt barely connected to my own sense of history. I think I lost it for a few months there because I was so tired and I didn't have any time to really reflect. I had been touring pretty consistently since 1985. I had no idea of how I wanted to present myself; I was experimenting wildly with my hair cuts! I was in my room with my scissors and I would get bored and would start snipping away and my hair started to go all askew, partly because I didn't want to be polished, and partly because I didn't want to present myself as some 'beautiful chick'. I wanted to maintain my perverse attitude and I wanted to see whether they would still accept me for my perversities.

In '86, we continued to tour and I'd gone right from these tours to working on the second album ['Solitude Standing'], because my manager could feel the momentum building and he was really pushing me to complete [it]. So I was aware of all this tension and by the time the whole thing broke in 1987, I was astonished. The album took off like a rocket – I wasn't expecting it at all. There was a huge buzz about 'Luka' before the album even came out; it went gold in eight weeks and we just toured the rest of the year. It was five shows a week, sometimes two shows a night, and all of them were sold out. We did tremendous business all over the world and it was really exhausting. [Our] car would even be mobbed!

'Luka' was unusual for that period in time, for it to be about child abuse and for it to be such an unqualified Top Ten hit almost everywhere in the world. My expectations of myself changed. I didn't know how to dress myself for a while. I felt really weird, because I always had a slightly idiosyncratic way of dressing anyway; it tended to all be from thrift shops; what I felt comfortable wearing was like, rags! So suddenly, when I was nominated for the Grammys, I thought, 'Does this mean I need to wear sequins and do my hair; what does this mean? How do I manoeuvre myself in this world?'

A lot of people want to know what the specific songs are about or how much is my own experience; what's this, or what's that, and how does it connect? And I figure that's my own business and maybe one day I'll write a book or I'll write something that will reveal that but right now I haven't written it and I don't really care what people think about it. People make all kinds of assumptions and that's fine because I've given them the stuff to do it with. I feel very strongly that I have my own particular thing that I'm working on that bugs me and keeps me going in a certain way and it's been at me for much longer than I've been in the public eye. When I read the horrible reviews, I think back to that time when I was in that club and the guy was eating his pork chop and drinking his beer and going, 'Look, hon, you've got really mellow songs but it's just not happening', and I just think, 'I know my own thread'. I don't pretend it's any more than that; it is my own particular thread that I'm on in the world and that's what I'm paying attention to and following.

Maybe at the end of your life, people will get some perspective but it seems stupid to make these judgements now when no one has any perspective on anything. I don't like what the media says for the most part. Respect, especially, seems very begrudging. So I read it once and then I put it away. Sometimes it's useful to me because I can see the reasons they're thinking this is because of what I've said, or what I haven't done, or the way I presented myself. It's that hard-nosed professional in me that says, 'OK, read this and figure out for yourself if what they're saying is true or not.' A lot of it is just, 'Oh, she's so thin and pale, we can sit and write things about her.' A lot of it is nothing to do with my real character, which is something they can't possibly know, because I haven't revealed it. And a lot of the songs are about hiding something . . . I expect people to do a certain amount of detective work and if they haven't done it, then they're left with an impression of someone who's kind of soft, and timid, which I'm not. If you start crying and taking it personally and writing letters to the press, then you're just done for.

I would say maybe four people in the whole world have asked me directly: 'Were you an abused child?' Most people will say, 'Did you know a Luka . . . Is there a real person that you know who was abused . . . Is there someone in your neighbourhood?', all those questions. So I find I don't answer it directly and I'll say, 'Yes, there was a boy named Luka, he was not abused, he lived upstairs from me and I just took his name because I liked it. I did know people who were abused' and that's all I say. I think what people need to know, they know already from the music, and those other people who don't need to know, it doesn't concern them. It says 'my name is Luka', it doesn't say 'my name is Suzanne Vega'.

The exciting thing about 'Luka' was that three million people heard that song and responded to it, and it had an effect in the world and people wrote to me about their own experiences. So for that moment, I was part of the world and part of the dialogue, which is thrilling and I loved it. I found, in a sense, that was more liberating than the money. It was really the feeling of having my own identity in the world that was the thrill, having the freedom to go wherever I wanted to go. And the feeling that I said something small, something in my room, but that three million people heard it and responded correctly. They knew the point that I was making. You get hooked on it, you want to do that all the time.

It was really June of 1988 before I could just sit down and take my breath because I'd been moving for two and a half years almost non-stop. I started to notice that there was all this stuff about Tracy Chapman and suddenly there's a lot of girls coming out and a lot of them seemed to stick my name to it. They said, 'Well, Suzanne Vega opened the door' and I'm sitting there going, 'I did?' So it was a short-lived feeling of being up on the peak for a minute. To watch Tracy Chapman's success was really stunning because she'd opened for me in some seedy little club in New Hampshire. Six months after that she was on the cover of *Rolling Stone*; her rise was spectacular and her sales were equally spectacular, whereas I think mine were still considered fairly alternative. She was really made into a symbol because she's a woman, she's black, she's political; she was just really thrown into the den.

When people said to me, 'Do you feel that you opened the door for these other women?', I had assumed that they were open and I was just walking through like everyone else, like Chrissie Hynde had done, like Joan Armatrading, like Joni Mitchell, like Rickie Lee Jones. I was aware that every one of these women had their own kind of talent and were probably doing that stuff since they were born and so they certainly weren't doing it thanks to me and I felt that having my name shoved in their faces was probably going to make them feel resentful towards me and that worried me, because I didn't like the idea of being the one held up as an example to be thrown rocks at. I didn't want to be remembered for having opened the door for other people; I wanted to be known for my own talent, my own nature, and for my own idiosyncrasies, and my own strengths.

In the beginning, ninety-nine questions out of a hundred were, 'So, you're obviously influenced by Joni Mitchell.' And I hadn't been. And it started to make me mad! But I think what's happening now is that there are so many women, that people are starting to make distinctions between them. I find that much more positive than jamming two women together in a closet and expecting them to sit comfortably together. Some days I was relieved, it was like, Tracy Chapman is taking the mantle of folk symbol. And I would also have the inevitable jealous feelings of 'Why does she get all the attention?' but I found that those feelings weren't useful for anything and to get myself out of that feeling I would just work. I bought Tracy Chapman's record, and Michelle Shocked's record and Tanita Tikaram's record and I listened to them and I would figure out what I liked and what I didn't like. That was a way of keeping it all in perspective. In the end I find it very peculiar that someone as different as Tracy Chapman and someone like Juliana Hatfield can both be compared to me and the two of them are completely different. At this point, it's all sunk down now and I feel I have some perspective on it.

I don't feel this thing of, 'I don't like women'; I like them, I want to get to know them, especially when they're doing cool things and expressing themselves in a man's world, because it's hard to do that. If you have any sense of compassion you have to get over that thing of wanting to be in the spotlight all the time and have it only on you. Because you're in the same boat as everyone else, whether you like it or not. You have to slug it out like everybody else That's why I think it's good that you have so many different women coming up now. Because each one is able to stand in her own light and be admired for her individual strengths.

There was all the pressure of that crazy year of 1987, all the fall-out in 1988 and so in '89 we were struggling to match up to what we'd done before and to surpass it. Also, to be surprising because I didn't want to make a record of ten socially-conscious songs with the acoustic guitar at the heart of it. I wanted to be challenging and I wanted to surprise people who thought they had me pegged. I think I did, even though ['Days of Open Hand'] didn't have nearly the effect that I had hoped that it would. In a lot of places, it just seemed like no one ever knew that it was out and some of that was because the record company had gone through tremendous upheaval. And, I have this very stubborn streak occasionally; I say, 'I know the right thing and I'm going to stick to it and to hell with you!' So that's the state of mind I was in. I probably could have done with a little more guidance but I think it was something that no one who was close to me felt that they could tell me. And they were right because I wouldn't have listened to them. So we then went on this ten-month world tour which was very difficult. The economy had taken a turn, my record company president had gone, I had a different A and R person who also left during that year. So, the company was falling apart, it was this ten-month endless odyssey all over the world, in a very different climate than the one three years before. I felt that I had taken a left turn and somehow it seemed so far left, that I was out of the ballpark.

I felt that one of the things that was wrong with the album was that, first of all, it didn't have enough contrast in it. It's too slow and careful and there's not enough spontaneity in it, even though I think it was a good job considering the pressure we were under and the conditions we were under. There's a lot of stuff I liked about the album but I decided for '99.9F' that I would go for wild extremes, that I would draw with a big fat crayon instead of little tiny pencil strokes. I wanted something that would be really startling and really direct and kind of cut through all of the ambience that I felt that people were starting to surround me with.

[Producer, Mitchell Froom] said something about revealing me to be the mutant that I really am, which is a funny comment but also very accurate because he just felt that to go the pure folk route wasn't going to work. So we put together these twelve songs with wildly different contrasts and textures and that was the first time that it really felt right to me, that I wasn't imitating someone, that I wasn't being less than what I really was. Because a lot of times on-stage I would feel that I was presenting myself to be a fraction of what I really could be, and that if I'd meet people face to face, they'd always say, 'Oh, she's not at all what we expected, she's not shy and introspective and glum.' So it was the first time that I really felt my true personality starting to come through.

I've gotten better at saying what it is that I want. Instead of just saying, 'Well, I don't hear any edge', I'm able to say, 'Let's turn this sound up, or get rid of that noise, or let's turn this fader up or . . . there's no high end.' You learn to say the words that correspond to the specific things.

When I first saw myself on television, or when I kept being confronted with these pictures of myself I felt annoyed because I felt that that had nothing to do with what my character was, and is. Because I feel that my character is very different from the way my face is or the way that I'm caricatured. I can understand why Sinead O'Connor would shave her head because you want to fight against that. I'm not creating an image. This is something that took me a long time to figure out; women have a bigger problem than men because women have to speak in that language of images and men are less likely to have to do that. If you look at Tom Waits or Leonard Cohen, both of them are iconoclastic, both of them go for that seedy elegance kind of look; they'll wear suits but they'll look like they've been sleeping in them. They can fit in anywhere. Whereas a woman doesn't have that same neutrality. A woman is either like a sex queen or a book-worm or something. I'd like to find that middle ground for a woman also, where you can be sexy, if you want to be, but you don't have to . . . I would like to have that way into the world that those men have where they can sit on a train and they're not hassled by anybody.

If you're going to stand on the stage, then you'd better give a show, and that was something that was hard for me to learn. You can't get on-stage and be pissed off because people are staring at you; if you don't want them staring at you, get off! If you get on-stage and cry, that's terrible, because then you're the amusement and if you're crying in front of a hundred thousand people, it becomes part of the act and that's horrible. I've had dreams where I try to sit in the audience and the spotlight keeps coming back at me and I go, 'No, stop, I'm watching the stage' and I'm saying, 'Well, it's not a very good show because there's nobody there.' It also makes me realise that I've chosen to be there.

Touring, there is tremendous pressure: you have to look good and be coherent and do the phoners [interviews] and worry about the ticket sales and figure out how to deal with that unruly heckler in the fourth row, and keep the rest of the audience interested, how to keep the band happy, how to keep the energy alive on-stage, how to keep your clothes clean and looking really good. And, figuring out which anecdotes to tell on-stage; figuring out the right lighting guy, firing someone if it goes wrong and always worrying about how the tickets are going to go, whether you're going to be able to break even in the end – whether it's all worth it! Sometimes I hate it, and sometimes I really love it. It's the challenge of it that keeps me going because it is exciting, especially when you can make it yield something, and make it work.

It's not a normal way to live, although I've been pretty happy with the way I am able to walk around and go shopping. I slide around as if I'm anonymous but occasionally, something will happen and I'll realise that people are watching me. If you're reading a book and someone comes up, demanding something, it can be kind of a pain but I find for the most part, it's easy for me to blend into wherever I am. I don't look for the attention and so I don't get it. Even if people know who I am, they don't come up. There are some days when I walk down the street and it's like I have a sign over my head and people are going, 'Oh, look, it's Suzanne Vega.' And there are other days when I can't get into my own gigs, or if I try to get into a club, my sister will walk through and they'll stop me and go, 'Yes, can I help you?' It's not something I can turn on and off; the light bulb comes on of its own free will sometimes.

My grandmother played in a lot of different bands and she played the vaudeville circuit in America. She was a drummer. My father, when I finally met him in '87, sent me all of these pictures of this woman at the drum-kit; she was in her twenties or thirties. My grandmother gave up my father for adoption and had put these three kids in an institution and carried on with her career. It was shocking to me, to come off the road in 1987 and have my father say to me, 'Well your grandmother was a musician on the road also.' It was a complete circle that I was not expecting at all, because I thought I was being all independent and unique. Music and the travelling seems to come through the bloodline.

Kirsty MacColl

Kirsty MacColl was born in Croydon, south London, in 1959, the daughter of playwright, folk singer and social activist, Ewan MacColl, and Jean Newlove, a choreographer and dancer. Her parents separated before she was born. She learned classical guitar and violin but grew up with the music of The Beatles, Neil Young, Frank Zappa and the harmonies of The Beach Boys, whose influence was later to be heard in her own multilayered vocal arrangements.

After leaving her south London school, she went to art college and, at nineteen, signed to Stiff Records. Her first single, 'They Don't Know', was well-received and was later an international hit for Tracey Ullman. She left Stiff for Polydor, where in 1981, she recorded her first album, 'Desperate Character', which included the hit single, 'There's a Guy Down the Chip Shop Swears He's Elvis'. She embarked on a hurried tour of Irish ballroom venues, an experience which was to give her a decade-long dread of live performance.

In early 1985, Kirsty MacColl's version of the Billy Bragg song, 'A New England', entered the British Top Ten on the day she gave birth to her first son. A hiatus in her own writing and recording followed, with the birth of a second son and a successful career as a session vocalist – with Talking Heads, The Smiths, Simple Minds, Happy Mondays, Billy Bragg among others – and songwriter for other artists, including Frida, formerly of Abba. MacColl's duet with Shane McGowan on The Pogues' 'Fairytale of New York' in 1987 has become a Christmas-time classic. It was her tour with The

Pogues which helped to dispel the stage fright she'd acquired seven years earlier.

She signed to the Virgin label and recorded 'Kite', a showcase album for her brand of literate, bitter-sweet and elegantly crafted pop music. The follow-up, 'Electric Landlady' – the title a spoof of the Jimi Hendrix album, 'Electric Ladyland' – was more successful in the United States, with the single, 'Walking Down Madison', about homelessness in New York City. Both albums were produced by her husband, Steve Lillywhite. Three years later, the album 'Titanic Days' (on the ZTT label) included the track 'Bad', a song about female revenge which included a tongue-in-cheek reference to the familial baggage that has followed her around: 'I've been the token woman all my life: the token daughter and the token wife.'

Among her television work, Kirsty MacColl has presented a BBC documentary on water pollution, and she appeared in her own, regular spot on the French and Saunders comedy series in 1990. Her writing for television included the title song to the Carlton comedy-drama series, 'Moving Stories'.

Kirsty MacColl lives in London with her two sons.

I was very keen on music from as far back as I can remember. It helped that I had a brother who was nine years older than me, so he was bringing things home that I'd get to hear. I remember hearing 'Good Vibrations' and playing it over and over again, thinking 'this is fantastic, I want to learn all the parts!' I must have been about four or five then. I was also very keen on The Beatles, who were still putting out albums every year at that point. It was always the biggest interest in my life, I don't remember being particularly interested in anything else. I was very ill a lot as a child, I always had really bad asthma and I never got to lead a really normal life. Music was a kind of release that you could just get lost in and it saved me from the outside world. I suppose I was quite unhappy in my own environment and it was the only thing that lifted my spirits and made me feel good.

When I was in my teens, I'd get home from school and go to my room and fiddle about on the guitar and try to learn loads of Neil Young songs. 'Harvest' was a really important album for me, it was one of the big milestones. I thought, '*This* is what I want to do, I want to write songs.' It was a major breakthrough for me. I was never just listening to one style of music, I was always influenced by anything I could lay my hands on. I went through various obsessions. When I was fourteen, I was very keen on maths and I was really into Bach at the same time. I went through a spate of listening to twenty-year-old rockabilly records and the Shangri-las. Obviously I got into a lot of stuff that was current, things like Steely Dan and The Ramones.

I don't ever remember my father living with us but I remember there was a very miserable atmosphere around so I think you inherit a bit of that. He'd bring his records over and leave them. I think I was so traumatised by my family, really, that I found it very hard to listen to anything that I associated with my parents. I couldn't really listen to folk music for many, many years. I didn't start listening to folk music until I worked with The Pogues. Also, I was very aware of the fact that he disapproved completely of anything that he regarded as commercial. It was a sort of sin really and there was probably nothing that his children could have done more to upset him than to want to become pop singers. The way I see it is that you write a song and the song isn't good or bad because of the arrangement, the song is either good or bad. The arrangement is just how you dress it up, it's the clothes it puts on when it goes out.

I was in an uncomfortable position because my father was very well-known to an older generation and there was a certain presumption among some people that I would be singing folk songs and doing *his* songs, and I was very determined to do my own songs, the way I wanted to do them. We were from completely different generations. My dad was quite old when I was born. As much as I loved him, I thought his outlook on what was valid and what was not was rather narrowminded. It just seemed to be dated, and slightly hypocritical. There are things about pop music that are good, you can have a message; ultimately, a good pop single transcends all that and that's why it's popular among millions of people. It's not preaching, it's uplifting.

I never thought we were competing in the same field because my dad was very politically active and would play to large folk audiences but a lot of those people would never go and see a pop gig. They'd never go and see David Bowie. Whereas I was coming from a different angle, I came out just as punk was happening and it was a completely different outlook, you didn't have to have spent fifty years learning [music] to go and do it.

I didn't grow up with my father and I didn't have the benefits (or not!) of seeing him on a daily basis but I'd get people coming backstage after gigs and talking very knowledgeably about him and it was very uncomfortable for me, because I didn't think I knew him as well as they thought they knew him. It was very hurtful and quite hard to deal with for a long time. It's funny really because as you get older, you realise that you've taken on more than you thought you had from your parents.

I was very naïve when I started. When I had my first single out in 1979 the record company wrote a press release without telling me. The first time I did an interview, somebody started asking me about my dad and I said, 'How do you know who my father is?' and they said, 'It's in your press release.' The record company had obviously thought, 'Let's angle it as, "it's in the genes, it's genetic music"', which is just a real insult. I wrote a teen ballad, I was a teenager at the time so that's what I did! What did that have to do with my parents?

They've [music writers] got to have some angle; they can't just say, 'Here's somebody doing their own thing, making the records they want to make.' It's never that straightforward, they'd rather see some Svengali in the background which is not necessarily true, but it's what people want to imagine, especially where women are concerned. Independent women make people nervous.

———————————■———————————

I've been making records for fifteen years and I started off much more malleable and much more eager to please because I figured all of these people at the record companies were at least ten years older than me and they must know what they're talking about. Then, after a while I thought, 'If they know so much, why aren't they making the records?' I thought, 'Maybe I do know what I'm talking about.' Since I realised that, I've been more and more determined to do it on my own terms, and not to be pushed around. Certainly, artistically, I make all my own decisions and if people don't like the records, then at least they don't like the records *I've* chosen to make. They're not listening to something that somebody else has created and I've just done the vocal on.

I don't know if I was particularly naïve or not, but I used to think that if you just kept as true to yourself as you could, it would be all right in the end. But I don't know if that's necessarily true. Because you can't say 'all the most sincere artists have the most success'. That's certainly not true but on the other hand, for me it would be worthless if I had a Number One record on someone else's terms. What's the point? It's not what I'm about. Also, because I feel that I've been swimming against the tide for so long now, the last thing I'm going to do is say, 'OK, I give up! What do you want me to wear?' I've really got nothing to lose now, and that's quite an empowering position to be in. It's not always easy but at least I feel braver, to a certain extent.

I think I did fairly well to carve my own niche because I don't fit into the stereotypical ideas of what a female pop-singer should be like. I'm not glamorous, I don't go in for dance routines (in public anyway!). All I want to do is sell enough records to enable me to make the next record, and that's the bottom-line. I really love doing it and I don't want to have to stop. It becomes harder and harder, the more determined you are to do it your own way. I never thought, 'I'd love to be on television, I must be a celebrity!' What I really want to do is just keep making music. It's uncharted territory because there aren't that many 34-year-old pop-singers who aren't glamour-pusses! I feel to a certain extent I'm on this personal crusade.

I think there are more women around now who don't conform to the original stereotypes, and that can only be good. There are still not that many in rock music – but Chrissie Hynde is the first and last rock icon for women to a certain extent. I'm like most women that I know: yes, I would like to be thinner but on the other hand, would it make my records/ job/life any better? And is it so important to me that I have to go off and spend two months starving myself just to suit some kind of pathetic image of what people think I'm about? I'm not earning the sort of money where I can stand up and say, 'Look, I'm doing just as well as those super-models!' But on the other hand I think it's good that women know that there are other women out there who are doing their own thing, without resorting to this ridiculous stereotypical behaviour and image. Nobody should feel forced to take on a completely alien persona in order to get the chance to be themselves, whether they are gay or heterosexual, or female or male.

Quite a few times in my career, I've suffered from not having someone around who could put things into perspective. To a certain extent, it was in the record company's interests that I wasn't too well informed because it made it easier for them to tell me to do things, and for me not to say 'no'. After a while I just kept finding myself doing these awful German television programmes, and thinking, 'What the hell am I doing here? I don't enjoy this, I'm not even getting the slightest bit of satisfaction out of it and I don't want to continue if it's under these circumstances.' So I retreated into my shell for a bit.

I got pregnant with my first son, and recorded 'A New

England' which was a hit, then I made a follow-up when he was a couple of months old. Then I got ill for a while and then I was pregnant again, so that meant about two years out. The reason I was working with other people was because I wasn't writing my own stuff when I was pregnant and I felt like all my brain cells had turned to jelly, so if I got a call from someone who I respected as an artist saying, 'we're making this record we'd like you to come and sing on this track', then I'd be glad to do it, because it felt like I was still alive!

It was fun because I did the best I could on one song or a couple of songs. They'd ask me because they'd want me to make up a vocal arrangement; they didn't ask me because they'd already got the parts and they just wanted me to sing 'doo-wop, doo-wop'! I got all the freedom that I have with my own stuff but I didn't have to worry about promoting it or dealing with a record company.

I was still writing but there's a world of difference between writing stuff and recording it, and having it released. I did a whole album that wasn't released, and when you've worked very hard on something for about eighteen months, you feel like you've had a baby and left it in a telephone-box. [The record company] didn't actually come down while we were recording it. I think they just decided that it was going to take too much effort to promote and they'd treat me as that year's tax loss! You get used to it. Every time things have got bad I think, 'Oh, no, this is terrible' and feel really dreadful for a few months but then afterwards, I just really want to kick arse, and get up and say, 'I'm going to show them!' And that's usually when I come up with my best stuff.

In 1989 'Kite' came about after my new-found confidence from touring with The Pogues. I'd gone from being pregnant twice and fairly housebound, and not doing so much, to being out on the road for a couple of months, living completely the opposite lifestyle and having all of this sudden freedom from domesticity. Because I hadn't written anything for quite a while I had lots of things burning to get out. I was pleased with that album. I thought it was a landmark as far as my writing went.

'Electric Landlady' didn't do as well as 'Kite' in the UK, it did better in America. It was the first record that I'd had released in the States, simultaneously with the UK. 'Madison' was the first thing I'd sung, not just written, that received some major air-play in the US. It's a completely different thing, America. It's a sort of animal on its own. Just to get something played on a regular basis on most of the relevant rock stations is a good thing. But it doesn't transfer to sales necessarily.

Charisma, in the US, which I was signed to, wanted me to go out and capitalise on the 'Madison' air-play. So we got a band together and rehearsed for three weeks, then we were told that we weren't getting the funding, the night before the first warm-up gig.

There were a number of things that probably contributed to that, partly the fact that [Virgin] were being bought out by EMI, and then they got rid of half of the artists roster and half of the staff, so I wasn't alone in that. I was just really unlucky in that it cost me, personally, lots of money.

It made me very determined to go on tour so I got another band together, with the help of Mark Nevin, and we went off round the UK and Europe under our own steam. I'd toured when I was twenty-one or so, after 'Chip Shop' came out. I'd done this tour of Irish ballrooms that was absolutely disastrous, and I was so terrified every night that it was just absolutely overwhelming. I couldn't cope with it at all, and that put me off for ten years. I didn't do any live stuff until The Pogues many years later. It was gigging with The Pogues that made me realise that it could actually be enjoyable, you could enjoy being on-stage. I'd never experienced that before, and I could never work out why people did it. I realised that there was a lot of fun involved as well, and also it gives you a completely new approach to singing. I became a better singer after working live a lot.

'Performing' is a word that is over-used. My vocals tend to be fairly deadpan, I tend to be more expressive with words than I am with delivery. It's that English [attitude]: 'Don't make a fuss, it's embarrassing!' I couldn't do all that screaming and bleeding on the carpet, I'm too reserved and shy for that. Although I was quite reserved about displaying emotion when delivering a song, it's a different thing to how I behaved in bars! I'm much too outspoken and mouthy to be a little English rose; I'm more Celtic in that sense. I've always felt more Celtic; my father was Scottish and my mother has Irish connections. All of the people I connect with best, artistically, have roots in the London or Manchester Irish scene.

When I did go out [on tour], it was because I'd said to myself, 'I'm going to book this up and if I don't enjoy it after two weeks, then I'll just not do it again.' I had to at least try it, I couldn't let my whole experience of touring amount to just one naff tour I did when I was twenty. After the first few gigs I was getting better every show we did, and enjoying it more, and it got to a point where some of the shows would be fantastic. You progress every time, you become more selective about what you think is a good gig.

Promoting 'Titanic Days', we were on tour in America for six weeks and I really enjoyed it. I had no idea what to expect. I knew we were playing smallish clubs but I didn't know if I'd have enough fans there or enough people who knew my work to even fill the clubs. So when I'd get to these places that I'd never been to before, in the middle of nowhere, and there'd be loads of people there, with loads of singles they'd got on import, it was quite a relief!

I like to make jangly, luscious, melodic pop music but with lyrics that are a bit more biting and down to earth than the average stuff you hear on the radio. For people who listen to music, they often enjoy that but I don't think the majority of people ever listen to the lyrics otherwise they wouldn't buy the records they do.

What I like to do, and what I enjoy about the people I enjoy listening to, is that they invest their energy into more real situations than a lot of the stuff that tends to get into the charts, which, if there are any lyrics, they're usually meaningless twaddle about 'oooh, baby, I can't live without you!' There are just so few people I know who can't live without somebody! It's just not true, is it? Women, especially, would always be singing these songs, when I was a kid; you'd hear them on the radio, and the songs were obviously written by a man and he was actually putting his words into the woman's mouth and he's making her out to be how *he* wants to perceive women, and not how women *are*. So where are all of these pathetic women who can't live without their man? I don't know any! A lot of the women I know tend to be the stronger partner in the relationship; they tend to be the one who is more reliable and they *have* to be. I think it's true to say that, generally, women can do ten jobs at once which is the main difference between them and men, because men tend to be able to do one thing at a time; they may do it well but they don't have to apply themselves to anything else.

People just assume that a woman should give up her career when she has children. You'd think that in the '90s they'd have gotten over this, but they still don't ever say, 'Has your husband taken a lot of time off since you've had the baby?' It's as if a man's career just carries on as normal and all these families come and go but he carries on. It's a bizarre concept really, that it should be so one-sided.

There are two ways of looking at it: You can say that you work in spite of having kids because you're incredibly selfish and maybe they're losing out because you're working but I tend to think that if I wasn't working, I'd be so bitter and twisted that they wouldn't want me around! They don't need me twenty-four hours a day, they're their own people now. They're well looked after and they see plenty of us, even if we're away for a few weeks of the year. They know they are loved. They've got their own lives, their own social lives, and school.

The reason that some people don't like your music is the same reason that other people do. So it's all so subjective. You can't say, 'If I change this, everybody will like it.' I think people appreciate the fact that I've stuck to my guns. I have experimented musically, I've worked with lots of different people and that's often gone against me in the music press because they think you're getting above yourself – you're working with foreigners! I just really enjoy the learning process and if I thought I didn't have anything left to learn, I'd just stop doing it. I like working with new people and trying different styles and pursuing different ends because it makes the whole thing much more enriching.

As far as 'Walking Down Madison' goes, I wrote the lyrics walking around in New York and a couple of years later I had still not managed to come up with any music for it. I tried out various ideas on my own. Then out of the blue I got a tape from Johnny Marr, saying, 'I came up with this idea, maybe you'd like to do something with it.' I thought immediately, 'I've already got the lyrics for this', so it was just a question of writing a melody in order to finish it. I thought that the funk-type, hip-hop approach worked because of the nature of the song lyrically, because it was set in New York and because it was very urban, and the rap influence. There is something about rap music that conjures up American cities more than European ones, or pastoral scenes.

There are three people that I've written a lot of material with – Johnny Marr, Pete Glenister and Mark Nevin. Johnny and Pete are superb guitarists/composers and Mark is also a lyricist in his own right, but they all give me chord progressions. We never write together in the same room at the same time. They've all been extremely supportive of me in times of chronic confidence shortage, as has Morrissey, and I love them all dearly. We all need support when self-doubt threatens to overwhelm us.

With Johnny, I do a lot of it by post because he's in Manchester and I'm in London. I'm quite lazy and it's good to have a catalyst. If I get a cassette in the post from one of them, I'll put it on and I'm away! There's something ready to go, whereas if I'm left to my own devices, and I think, 'I might start fiddling around on the guitar today', I may or may not come up with something at the end of it. It's quite a lonely business, song-writing, and the joy of writing with someone else is to have someone to bounce ideas off and to have input from another angle.

It's certainly a talent and probably an art in itself, but I can't identify with that Tin Pan Alley approach to song-writing where you go in at nine o'clock in the morning and write a song before lunch, then write another one in the afternoon. There are a lot of people who do that successfully, who can work that way; I'm not one of them.

I get regular writer's blocks and the times when you are writing a lot are not always the times when it's most convenient to write. Usually when there's a lot going on, you don't write about it when it is going on, you wait until that's subsided and in the days that follow, that are more calm, you sometimes have more time to think about it and write about it. I find that once I get on a roll, I can't stop writing. I try not to panic about the blocks now because I don't think the panic helps the process, it just makes the block longer and more tedious and more traumatic. I just think, 'OK, it's not happening today' and I do other things. I might be recording or working on some music and not coming up with any lyrics. I just wait till it starts happening again, really. I haven't found the magic potion that turns it on.

Pop music is the natural habitat of the supremely superficial but 'pop' can cover a broad spectrum, and for every hundred disposable, inane songs there is one that strikes a chord with people, whether it is about pain and confusion, or nothing much at all!

There's a fine line that you have to tread – there tend to be an awful lot of songs written about the homeless, by people who only drive around in limos and probably don't really see them unless they're about to run them over as they leave a club! I'm not a spokeswoman by any means but I don't think you can walk around any major city and not be aware of it; I don't see how it can not cross your mind.

I feel lucky that I'm still able to make records whether or not I can make them here; or just in America, I *can* make records and that's as much as I can hope for. In the face of all the overwhelming evidence to the contrary – that you have to look a certain way, and behave a certain way and promote things in a certain way – I still get a chance to be myself. You always feel that every record could be your last, because if you don't sell enough, no one's going to give you money to make the next one.

I see my career as a long-term thing and it's been going fifteen years now, but I've had so many different record companies, it feels like I've got a new one every six months! They don't all, obviously, see my career as long-term as I do. As long as I feel I really enjoy it and get a lot out of it, I'm going to continue doing it, whether they want me to or not. I feel it's my duty to out-wit them at every opportunity!

If you really believe that what you're doing is basically good stuff then you have to carry on with it. And if you're not sure, then you should just give up. And most people do give up. That's why there are not that many people still around who've been doing it for fifteen or twenty years. Some people might have a hit single or one hit album, and they'll probably last about five years. It is hard to keep it going. That's what separates the women from the girlies!

Nanci Griffith

© ROCKY SCHENK/COURTESY MCA

Nanci Griffith was born in Austin, Texas, in 1953. She grew up listening to the music of folk legends like Odetta, Woody Guthrie and Pete Seeger, and although struggling with dyslexia, began to write her own songs at the age of ten. Inspired by the singing of Carolyn Hester and Bob Dylan, she began performing in clubs when she was fourteen. She continued performing after she went to the University of Texas, where she gained a degree in education. After leaving college, she taught first grade – five- and six-year-olds. A local singer, Eric Taylor, introduced her to the folk circuit in Houston and Austin; they later married. The marriage failed, as an increasingly violent Taylor battled against drug problems.

Nanci Griffith spent the next ten years touring the United States, booking her own shows and driving herself from town to town. In 1978, she recorded her debut album, a live set of largely self-penned folk-inspired songs, 'There's a Light Beyond These Woods', on B.F. Deal Records. This was followed four years later with 'Poet in My Window', co-produced with John and Laurie Hill, on the Featherbed label. The following two albums, on Philo/Rounder, received widespread critical acclaim: 'Once In A Very Blue Moon' (1984), co-produced with Jim Rooney, featured a guest appearance by Lyle Lovett on a cover version of his 'If I were the Woman You Wanted' and 'The Last of the True Believers' (1986), which earned Nanci Griffith her first Grammy nomination for Best Folk Album. The album includes 'Love at the Five and Dime', based on a short story Griffith had written years earlier; the song proved a huge hit on the country charts when it was covered by Kathy Mattea. The album's success clinched a deal with the major label MCA Nashville, and in June that year Nanci Griffith began recording in Nashville with co-producer Tony Brown, who had signed her to MCA.

The following year, her MCA debut, 'Lone Star State of Mind', included an early cover of Julie Gold's classic, 'From A Distance'. In 1988, another Griffith-Brown co-production, 'Little Love Affairs', sold well in Britain after Griffith toured there. In August of that year, her performances at the Anderson Fair club in Houston were recorded for release as 'One Fair Summer Evening'. Griffith's US chart debut was marked the following year with 'Storms', produced by Glen Johns and featuring guests such as former Eagle Bernie Leadon, Albert Lee and Phil Everly. The album went to number 38 on the UK album chart, and number 99 in the US.

In September 1991, she released 'Late Night Grande Hotel', produced by Rod Argent and Peter van Hooke, who were chosen after Griffith heard their co-production, Tanita Tikaram's 'Ancient Heart' album. 'Late Night' featured a guest appearance by Tikaram and a duet with Phil Everly. The album perplexed US radio programmers, unable to decide which category best suited Nanci Griffith's genre-defying music – folk, rock, or country. It was to be her last album with MCA Nashville.

Griffith's immense popularity in Ireland was boosted in 1992 with her appearance on The Chieftains' album, 'The Bells of Dublin', to which she contributed 'The Wexford Carol'. Their earlier collaboration, 'An Irish Evening Live at the Grand Opera House, Belfast, With Roger Daltrey and Nanci Griffith', won a Grammy for Best Traditional Folk Album. In October, Griffith took part in the all-star tribute to Bob Dylan, singing 'Boots of Spanish Leather' with one of her folk heroes, Carolyn Hester.

In early 1993, she moved from MCA to Elektra in the United States, and recorded 'Other Voices, Other Rooms' (named after a book written by Truman Capote). The album was a loving and ambitious tribute to her musical heroes, with cover versions of her favourite songs – featuring artists such as Carolyn Hester, Odetta, Bob Dylan, Chet Atkins, Emmylou

Harris, John Prine, Arlo Guthrie, Guy Clark and The Indie o Girls. It won a Grammy for Best Contemporary Folk Album. It was followed in October 1993 by a 'Best of . . .' compilation, which featured previously unreleased material as well as highlights from seven albums.

'Flyer', her twelfth album, was released in September 1994. It featured a duet with Counting Crows singer Adam Duritz, 'Going Back to Georgia', which he also co-wrote; two other tracks were produced by Peter Buck of REM and musicians making guest appearances included U2's Adam Clayton and Larry Mullen Jr, Mark Knopfler, Emmylou Harris, The Chieftains and The Indigo Girls.

Nanci Griffith lives in Nashville, Tennessee.

———————————————— ■ ————————————————

My parents were beatniks so I had a rather eclectic choice of music to listen to in the house: everything from my dad's taste in folk music – The Weavers and Odetta – to my mother's interest in jazz, Frank Sinatra and Count Basie. I don't really remember finding anything that I latched on to as being part of my life until Janis Ian and Bob Dylan came along, or going back and listening to my older sister's Everly Brothers records. Those things became a part of my life as opposed to just adopting the tastes of my parents.

They were great parents, they really tried to give us an interest in doing something with our lives as adults. My parents thought you had to be busy doing something productive all of the time. Even though it was a great Dr Spock idea, in reality it drove us crazy as children, having someone wanting us to be productive all the time!

Now, when I'm around small children I try to allow them that space; every once in a while you see a child just standing there and you know that something's going on in there. Having been a school teacher of young children, of five-year-olds and six-year-olds, I would realise that if you asked the child what they were actually doing, they couldn't tell you. They wouldn't even know what they were thinking about because they were someplace else.

Life was really confusing for me when I was four and five years old, that's when [dyslexia] really starts to manifest itself, when you're trying to learn things that are linear and you're a global person, it's really difficult. My grandmother was very understanding. She was a teacher and she had studied dyslexia, even though it was before her time, she understood that it was a real problem, and it wasn't me being stupid. So she took me to the University of Texas and I was in a special programme and they followed me all the way through school until I was eighteen years old. So I did learn how to read in a way that I could read, and do things in my own way. It's still confusing, there are some things that will always be a problem. I misread road signs, I misread recipes, math I'm terrible at, balancing my chequebook is an extreme headache for me. I think from what I read and learn about dyslexia, and it's what I studied in college as well when I was going into teaching, is that the most creative people in the world have been dyslexic!

I wanted to be able to help other children with the same problem and I think that just as the best drug counsellors are people who've had drug problems, it's the same thing with a learning handicap. I think that someone who has lived through it and gone beyond it is much more capable of understanding the frustration of a child who is just trying to learn their own system of working their way round it. I really enjoyed teaching, enjoyed the children. I was just overwhelmed by their capabilities, their openness. They're just driven to learning how to read, how important that is. When you've around thirty children a day who are that involved in learning how to read, it makes you remember how much it meant to you. We tend to take it for granted as adults. It opens a whole new world of imagination to them.

I never pursued a musical career so much as I was just in love with music and loved playing music. Then and now, I would meet artists, and there seemed to be two different types . . . the artist who had an interest only in being famous and then the artist who had an interest in and a love of music. I fall in that category of being in love with music and not interested in that other thing; I really did not want that other thing because it interfered with what I could do musically.

I didn't particularly care for really rowdy places but it was a challenge to learn the art of changing that rowdy atmosphere, of convincing people that they came into that bar to hear music and that they *would* go home having enjoyed themselves. So that was a challenge and had I not grown up in central and west Texas, I would have never learned that. It's a challenge and some nights you lose and some nights you win but I'm deeply grateful for that challenge because I've never forgotten it, and I don't take for granted anything when I walk out on stage.

The stage is sacred, and it's *my* space, it's the only space on earth that's really mine. When I walk out there on that stage, every person out there is important, every one of them is an individual to me, they're not just an audience, they're not just three thousand, five thousand people – they're one individual and each one of them put their hand in their pocket and paid to come and hear my music. That's overwhelming to me, and I have a great responsibility to them. So, I respect artists who say 'I don't owe my audiences anything, I did this myself, and if they don't like what I'm doing this time, or this record, or this tour, that's too bad', but I feel an obligation to the audiences, even though I'm not going to change what I do if they don't particularly care for a genre of music that I'm exploring, I still feel obligated to them. I owe them everything, they've made Nanci Griffith, I didn't make myself, audiences made me, musically.

It took some of the horror and strain of being on the road as a woman by myself, driving myself around America, if I could plan my own touring schedule so that I could be in Minneapolis when an old friend was going to have a birthday, or I could be in the west when the desert was in bloom, little things that I could do for myself to make it not seem so businesslike but to make it seem an adventure and a learning process and fun. And

I've tried to continue that. Even though now when we're on tour we have this huge entourage, all the band members and crew, I still say, 'We're going here, let's make a field trip and do this!' We'll all go to the zoo together, or we'll go to look at some ruins, wherever we're going to go, just find someplace and have fun.

You have to have a life and I've never really had what I consider a *life* like most people's but that has become a life, my road-life is combined with my life. Because I've stayed on the road most of my life, I've never concentrated on having a family, because when I was younger I couldn't afford to have a family, so I didn't have one. Now, I'm not sure that I have what it takes to have that discipline. I'm so accustomed to working this way by myself, so I think it is the 'road less taken'.

Since I've never been an overnight sensation, there's never been a 'flavour of the month' label attached to me. Each record has sold better than the last, each tour has gotten larger than the one before it, and I think that'll continue to happen, until I decide that it's time to take a break. I was already established as an artist, and had already established myself with four albums on independent labels, which had sold very well, and tours that had done well and I think that saved me from ever having that manipulation from record labels: 'Oh, Nanci Griffith didn't have a hit off that album, we're either going to have to drop her or change her image, change her hair, change the type of music! What are we going to do with her?' Because I was already an entity, I'm just an entity, I don't fit into any particular place, I just am what I am.

George Thorogood and myself were, and still are, the two largest selling artists that Rounder ever had but I think that there were no expectations for me for commercial success from the very beginning, even before I made my first album. What I do has not been a commercially viable thing for so many years. I had role models who certainly paved the road for me and even if it is the 'road less taken', I'm certainly not the pioneer of it. People came before me: Janis Ian, Carolyn Hester, Emmylou Harris, they were all there doing the hard part. So I never really expected any sort of commercial success, I did expect to be a successful songwriter, but as an artist myself, because I am uniquely different in this slot of how I sound, of what my voice is, of what my guitar playing is, the eclectic choice of music that I explore, I never expected any sort of commercial success for myself. I've exceeded my expectations of what I thought I would achieve.

I really respect people's individuality and resented anyone thinking that I had purposefully tried to emulate anything. I'm not skilled enough to emulate anything, I can only be what I am. Lots of artists can adapt and sing different things, and do different things but I'm just me, that's it. If you want me to sing on your record, to back-up harmonies or play rhythm guitar don't expect it to sound like Trisha Yearwood singing back-up because it's going to sound like Nanci Griffith!

In pop and country music, for the last few years, I think the best records have been made by women, and I think there's even more pressure on men, especially in country music. I just find it a dreadful time in country music right now with all of this pressure for every young male country performer, whether he's a songwriter or not, to either be Dwight Yoakam or Garth Brooks.

We just came through a time when every label was trying to sign up every female singer-songwriter and I'm so glad that I was successful before that happened, and on my own little gravel road out there, driving around, instead of being caught up in that. Where are those women now? They got signed up, they were put in this pigeon-hole and several of them had one or two huge hits and then they were gone. They hadn't built a career, they hadn't built a loyal following. I'm deeply grateful that that didn't happen to me. It's all timing, and it's through no fault of their own, or lack of talent. It was just being pigeon-holed. There are some things in failure to be grateful for!

A few years ago I went through a depression of sorts, because I was just looking at other things too much; it was right in the middle of that 'OK, every label is going to sign every woman singer-songwriter on earth' time and I was watching people who I had known just fly by me on the highway, so to speak. While I was very happy for them and I was not envying their success, I was depressed because of what I considered the lack of my own. My manager kept telling me, 'You've got to start looking at what you've done. You were creeping along like a little turtle, and you opened a lot of gates and doors which allowed that to happen.' I couldn't see it then. He said, 'At the end of the day, when you get to the finish-line, you'll still be going.' And it's proven to be true.

Women are taught, from Day One, to compete against each other anyway. Whereas men are taught to work in teams, women are taught, 'You have to be prettier than the girl next door, you have to be better, and no matter how you get there, you have to get the man!' Because I've lived my life for the past twelve or thirteen years just in solitude, really without being much involved in anything, I don't have that feeling; I lost it. Maybe I had it before I was married but it went away! I don't feel like I'm competing against anyone; the only person I'm competing against is myself. I have to create a better piece of work than I created the last time. I have to grow and I have to be continually learning and continually bettering myself in some way, mentally.

I was fortunate to come to the major label industry with an identity that no one really wanted to change or tamper with, and every label that I've worked for has allowed me to run amok, and to do exactly what I wanted to do. I don't think the thought ever crossed their minds, that someone's going to have to tell Nanci Griffith that she's going to have to change the way she dresses or she's going to have to change her sound, because so-and-so's popular right now and she's going to have to match that.

———————————————■———————————————

I've gone through different phases of writing, different ways to an end, as far as approaching writing. ['Flyer'] has been very unusual, because in years past, my writing has been very fictional, very story-oriented. People interpreted it as being Nanci Griffith but if I'd lived all of those lives, it would have been a very hard life indeed! ['Flyer'] is almost like my Thomas Wolfe album, because it's very personal, it's very immediate; something would hit me and I'd write about it as opposed to, as Harlan Howard once described my writing, 'When Nanci does write a song, she's the one who writes it down but it's going to be five years from now before you see it come before you and then you won't recognise yourself anyway.'

There is a piece of me in all of my writing. I'm going to try as much as I can, as a writer, to be journalistic but my opinion is always going to be there. People are always going to be able to judge what kind of person Nanci Griffith is, by my writing. And that's probably what I consider to be a small flaw in my ability to write. It bothers me sometimes when people come up and they'll quote a line of mine to me, because I don't remember it! They expect it to be a catch-phrase, that I should immediately have this propinquity with this person because of that phrase. So that's a bit disconcerting, when someone thinks they have you down that much.

I've admired so many writers that I really don't have a true sense of their person, because they were so brilliant at writing fiction. Like Tom Waits, I don't have any clue as to who Tom Waits is, because he is such a brilliant writer. If I didn't know her as a friend, I wouldn't have any clue what Suzanne Vega is like, as a person, she's such a brilliant writer. I admire that type of writer, the existentialism of being able to do that. I can't do that! I'm too involved with a piece of work.

I've brought an objectivity to certain things . . . you either had bitter angry women shouting at you on one side or you had 'Stand by your man'. I've written about abuse and I've written about surviving it, written about getting up and walking away, getting into the Ford Econoline and driving away. And not in a bitter way but in a way of overcoming this. I think women can relate to that because it's true. It's closer to the reality of what process you actually go through in life.

I did have a hard life, I did have a hard marriage, I was abused. I was married to a brilliant man, a brilliant writer who was also a drug addict and a Vietnam veteran who had lost his innocence to that war. I was too innocent to understand that.

I've never blamed him, we're dear friends. He's a psychologist now, and a different man. Overcoming the damage that abuse causes, especially if you came from a background that was totally opposite, is a life-long process and I continue to write about it in forms that are not so blatant; they're not protest songs, they're healing songs. I know, from letters that I get, that they have helped other people and if I have the ability to write something like 'I Wish it Would Rain' or 'Listen to the Radio' or 'Fragile', a song that changes one person's life, or gives the car-keys to one woman, or gives her the ability to change her life, then I've done something that is a blessing to me.

Most of my friends say I'm living my twenties now because I didn't have any twenties. The years of my twenties and thirties were spent in a very grim situation; that's not to say I didn't learn from it and that it won't be a basis for the kind of person I'll be for the rest of my life. I did not experience any kind of youthful hoopla so I'm really having a second childhood now!

I think I've used and manipulated my writing to help myself and to work through problems within myself. It's not that I'm a particularly spiritual person. I have a friend who talked me into having my cards read, I'd never been before, I'd never done anything like that. This person I went to was particularly good, she didn't know me but she said, 'You've had a really, really hard life, this is really painful to look at but you've done a lot of work, you've done all the inner work and you're through with that now. The rest of your life, you can have a good time, you deserve it!' It was fun and it also gave me the licence to have a good time!

I had written a short story about this couple, Eddie and Rita, in college and I just took it and did the song ['Love at the Five and Dime']. It came very quickly and I never thought I would do it again. There've been a lot of songs like that, that have just popped out for one reason or another and have ended up being big songs for me. I always felt that if I couldn't remember it [a song] nobody else could. I don't write it down until somebody says, 'can I have a lyric sheet' and I'll type it up. I never write anything down. I don't keep a journal, I don't 'save' lines. They just come and they go. If they come out in a great way, that's fine. If they don't, that's OK too.

I used to be very disciplined about my writing. I used to get up every morning and write, before anything interfered with the thought process. I don't do that any more, I'm not very disciplined. I'll set a deadline for myself, because I write for other people: I've got to have ten songs finished and out six weeks from now. Once I've set that, I'll get to work and get it done. It makes me kind of multi-personalitied, because one side would say, 'OK, I'm going to be doing a record of my own in a year and I need to be writing for that', and the other part of me is saying, 'So-and-so is doing an album, they've asked me for material and I've got to have it for them because they're depending on me to write it.' It's almost like two different lives.

I'm really frightened of losing control of the visual image that's placed behind my songs, because I've never wanted a storyline video, simply because it interferes with my audience's imagination. It's why I became a writer, to give people three and a half minutes of someplace else to go and someone else to be. So, video can really interfere with that. The only time I've ever done any kind of storyline was with 'Speed of the Sound of Loneliness', with John Prine and I being angels because both of us had been so heavily influenced and our lives changed by Wim Wenders' [film] *Wings of Desire*. We wanted to do something along those lines that did not have anything to do with the stories but was just a visual image.

———————————————————◼———————————————————

Because of my allergy to country-music radio, and my dislike of the way that the established country-music business works, I never wanted anything to do with country music. Even though I write country music, it's a part of me as a writer, it's a part of my heritage, part of my roots.

All of a sudden I was [labelled] a New Country artist. I ran for the hills when that was placed on me! The first time I read it, was in NME in London; NME had always been exceptionally supportive of me. I said, 'I will not be part of it!' because I had gone out of my way in Europe, Great Britain and Ireland, not to be part of it. It was a real shock when I was included. It's over now I think and I think the point was made well: I just disappeared for a year, I refused to give interviews, I refused to talk about it if someone asked me to say what I thought of a New Country artist, I'd just say, 'I don't know, I don't listen to it, so why ask me?' It went away but it took a while.

When I was just getting my foothold playing music, I didn't know who Rosanne Cash was until I turned on the radio one day and I never listened to country music, because it was like the 'Urban Cowboy' era of country music and I hated that. I just happened upon Rosanne Cash and 'Seven Year Ache' but she was played on country radio, she wasn't played on pop [stations]. It was so odd to hear her played in that format, I thought 'this doesn't belong here!' I became a fan and bought her records.

Loretta Lynn was a major influence on me; in pop music and country, whichever genre you choose, there is such a small handful of women songwriters. There are lots of women singers but there are so few songwriters. And it hasn't changed. If you look at the Top Twenty in country music right now, you'd find Joie White, you'd find Mary Chapin Carpenter and you'd find Suzy Boguss. I can't think of anyone else. The rest are singers. There's still that gap there.

[1994] is the second year in a row that no women have been nominated for the Rock and Roll Hall of Fame. When is Carole King going to be in the Rock and Roll Hall of Fame? Or Laura Nyro? It's unbelievable! They got blasted for it last year. Who does these nominations anyway? It's so blatant and it's become a joke, because it's so unfair. Certainly all of the artists who have been inducted into the Rock and Roll Hall of Fame belong there. I'm not taking anything away from the talent of those men but . . . when are they going to realise that people are not going to give this organisation any kind of credibility until they stop being that way.

The industry put 'bad word' around folk music for twenty years. That was one of the major pushes on me to make 'Other Voices, Other Rooms' because I was just tired of that [attitude]. I was tired of people being afraid of being called a folk artist, because their [record] label would make that a bad word. That's what I am and I'm proud of it, I'm proud of my heritage and proud of my heroes. Not only that, they're *great* people. Odetta is the most magnificent person on earth, Carolyn Hester, Pete Seeger, are all brilliant people. They created an art form and I don't ever want to have to deny them, or where I come from. Bob Dylan is an idol, I can hardly put a sentence together when I'm around him! And he's a lovely man. Folk music is here to stay and every generation is going to create their own folk revival in their own way. With our generation, we have U2 and REM and The Indigo Girls who are carrying on a whole folk revival of their own, on a whole different level, and it's still folk music.

If you're secure in who you are and what you are, good and bad, then you don't mind saying 'look over there!', you don't mind turning the flashlight on somebody else because you're not going to go away, people aren't going to stop looking at you because you've turned the light on someone else. A lot of those other artists know who their influences are but they refuse to acknowledge them and it infuriates me. They can't say, 'Look at that, *that's* the real thing!' When in doubt, go to the source. Someone like Iris de Ment, her influences were people like myself and Emmylou [Harris], artists who had a difficult time establishing themselves and she is going to have a hard time, without the support of other people, the lending of their name, she might not get heard and it's important to me, for her to get heard. It's just a matter of sharing; if I hear something great, I want to pass it on.

I've never been considered a political artist but I know that I am. I had a young artist, who is always in trouble about politics, and she'd just gotten in big trouble over something she had said, and she asked me, 'How come you never get in trouble, every time I see you, you go out on stage and tell a joke or flip something by there and everybody says "yes, that's true", nobody gets up in arms about it, nobody writes about it.' I said, 'It's like that line in *Fried Green Tomatoes*; "I'm older, I'm wiser, I have better insurance!"' And I speak very softly: 'Speak softly but carry a big stick!' I'm not going to yell at anybody, it does no good; I'm not just going to play for my political peer group. I want to play for that person that I disagree with, without them knowing that I disagree with them, and hopefully a little bit of something will click in as they leave the building. I think I'm very radical politically but I don't often get in trouble for it. No one responds to being shouted at, no one does; it doesn't work. You have to at least carry on some facade of being involved in the other person . . . there have been times when I've been wrong and that facade has fallen away and I've learned from that person who I thought was so wrong.

I so rarely do a benefit of any kind. I just don't get involved in 'causes'. Any kind of organised 'anything', I don't particularly care for. I think that's the difference between people's reasons for doing these organised things; a lot of times, their reasons are that career thing, as opposed to being in love with this music or this cause.

I've been on college radio and alternative radio my entire career, and that's not mainstream pop radio or mainstream country. It's only just now become fashionable to be on adult-alternative radio or college; five years ago, it was not fashionable to be on independent radio but now that's what artists want. It's the kiss of death to be on pop radio! It's a change in people's tastes. You can't listen to something you've never been exposed to. Radio, I think, has always controlled the record industry and not the other way around. No matter how hard the record industry tries to control radio, they're never going to do it. I find radio in England to be extremely powerful. Every single that's released rests entirely on whether it will be played on [BBC] Radio One.

MCA just forgot to submit me for Grammys five years in a row; if your label doesn't submit you, you're not nominated. So I was very depressed in general . . . My first record for Elektra, 'Other Voices, Other Rooms', was nominated for a Grammy and it won. As my manager told me, 'It's not your station in life, it's where you're stationed!' Even though I'm honoured that I won the Grammy, I was certainly honoured to win the IRMA award in Ireland and very proud of winning the Edison Award the year before, and awards in Europe and Britain. I'm very proud of all of the awards I've won but because I had all those years where I was not submitted for a Grammy, I had to live with questions from my family, who don't understand the politics of it . . . because I had all of those years, I know the politics of it and although it's a great honour, it's not going to affect what I do or how successful I consider a piece of work to be.

My measure [for success] is getting a wonderful letter in the mail that says, 'I did this because of something that you wrote' or a confirmation from a peer, someone that I deeply respect, having Bob Dylan say, the first time I met him, 'I really liked your "Once in a Very Blue Moon" album.' I thought, 'He knows who I am, that's wonderful!' Those things mean a whole lot more to me.

Neneh Cherry

© EDDIE MONSOON/COURTESY RMP

Neneh Cherry was born in Stockholm, Sweden, in 1964. Her Swedish mother, Moki, an artist, and her father Ahamadu Jah, a percussionist from Sierra Leone, divorced when she was a baby. Her mother married the American jazz trumpeter, Don Cherry, and the family divided their time between Sweden and New York. She often travelled with her parents while they performed the multi-media Organic Music Theatre shows, and when Cherry toured with other jazz performers such as Carla Bley, Art Blakey and Pharaoh Saunders.

She left school at fourteen and the following year her father took her back to Africa to meet his family – an experience she later described as 'overwhelming'. She went to London in 1980 to accompany her step-father and his band on a tour with the all-women punk band The Slits, and dub artist Prince Hammer. She decided to stay in London and joined the jazz-funk band Rip, Rig and Panic. She became involved with RRP drummer Bruce Smith, and at eighteen, Neneh Cherry gave birth to their daughter, Naima. After recording three albums on the Virgin label, Rip, Rig and Panic broke up and some of the members, including Cherry, formed the band Float Up CP. Cherry began to rap at a London club – which paid five pounds a night to its rappers – and, while there, was spotted by a record company executive who encouraged her to record a single of her own. It became 'Stop the War', which was about the Falklands/Malvinas conflict. The B-side of the single was 'Give Sheep a Chance', a salute to the island's sheep population which far exceeds its human population.

She began a personal and professional relationship with Cameron McVey, a photographer and videomaker who had founded the band Morgan McVey. Through McVey, she became part of the 'Buffalo posse' clique of stylists, photographers and models who gathered around the designer Ray Petri. The 'Buffalo' style was later to typify Cherry's strong 'street-style' image, and gain imitators on both sides of the Atlantic. Cherry and McVey prepared to launch her solo recording career, creating a new musical style of rap and soul, with the help of drum programmer Phil Chil. The team produced demo recordings which garnered interest from several recording companies, including Circa, which eventually signed Cherry.

Her first album, 'Raw Like Sushi' – a hybrid of soul, rap and funk music, produced by McVey under his 'Booga Bear' moniker – was released in June 1989, and went on to sell more than two million copies worldwide. The first single off it, 'Buffalo Stance', reached the Top Ten in Britain and the US. The single, produced by Tim Simenon, was released a month before Cherry gave birth to her and McVey's daughter, Tyson. The video for the follow-up single, 'Manchild', featured Cherry holding her baby daughter.

For the next three years, she worked on a variety of projects. In late-1990, the 'Red Hot and Blue' compilation of cover versions of Cole Porter songs featured her rendition of 'I've Got You Under My Skin'. It was one of the most successful singles from the album, which raised money for AIDS research. In 1990, Rip, Rig and Panic reunited briefly to play at a memorial concert for their bass-player, Sean Oliver, who had died suddenly. Cherry and McVey set up their Cherry Bear production company and produced the 'Blue Lines' album for the British rap group Massive Attack.

In 1992, Cherry and McVey, now married, moved to Sweden – to Cherry's childhood home at Hassleholm – to record her second album, 'Homebrew'. The album was produced by Cherry, McVey and Johnny Dollar. It featured samples from Steppenwolf and Led Zeppelin, guest appearances from Lenny Kravitz and Gang Starr and a duet with REM's Michael Stipe on

'Trout' which called for better sex education in schools. As Neneh Cherry wrote for her follow-up album in mid-1994 she shared a British Top Ten hit with Youssou N'Dour when she duetted on and co-wrote his single, 'Seven Seconds'.

Neneh Cherry lives with her husband, Cameron McVey, and their two daughters in London.

I grew up around so much music that it was kinda just like food and I always really loved music. A lot of the things that I loved the most were just there in my house. My dad bought Sly and the Family Stone, he bought the first Jackson Five record. They weren't really things that I went out and got myself but I used to listen to those records every single day. I never actually managed to learn how to play an instrument, my dad would try to show me how to play the piano; I would lose my patience and I would kick the piano stool over. I never really felt like I could do it, I probably didn't have the confidence in myself until I started listening to X-Ray Spex. Poly Styrene's voice was actually the first voice that I could really sing with. Then one day my dad was playing 'Put another Nickel in the Nickelodeon' and I remember singing it like Poly Styrene and it really worked. I was about thirteen or fourteen.

I left school, not really to leave school but because I was not in a good frame of mind and things weren't working out. I was in Sweden and I went to New York and I was going to go back to school and then things just happened. I was just rebelling against everything because I was so unsatisfied, but I think that it also gave me this sense of urgency. I was very self-conscious of the things that I didn't know because I had left school, and so I always did quite a lot to catch up, read a lot, I pushed myself. I think that's maybe why things came to me.

I started playing bass, I sang backing vocals with this weird pseudo-ska band called The Nails in New York when I was fifteen. I left my family and went to London when I was sixteen. Then I was asked to join Rip, Rig and Panic and I became part of something that I could really identify myself with. The music was jazz-inspired and they paid homage to a lot of musicians that I had grown up with.

But when it came to doing my own thing – I hate to call it my own thing because everyone that has been part of it has been such a big part of it – it had to be something else. Cameron said, 'why don't we try rap' because he knew how much I was into it. I probably wouldn't have thought of it myself. I used to go out to clubs and rap for a fiver, so I could go out and do the shopping the next day. There really weren't that many women around doing it, not in the way that we were doing it.

From the first time that I heard rap, it's been a really big part of my life. The first rap record that I had was called 'Vicious Rap' by this female called Sweet T, Tanya Winley. It was just brilliant, it was a band playing and it was just really aggressive, it just starts out with this siren, and then hearing a female voice just being there. For me, rap was very 'male' for a long time and it was tough for a woman to break into it. I'm a contradiction, by no means am I a rap artist but that has been a real saving grace, so has reggae, so has punk.

My jazz heritage has become something that I can relate to and tap into now much more than then. Then, it was just like an education that I had. We would travel a lot and my mum and step-dad really wanted to keep the family together as a family. They called [their show] the Organic Music Theatre. It was about music from all different parts of the world, merging that with his heritage, with what he did, and he was constantly learning and discovering. The more you listen to it, and the more you become accustomed to very different kinds of music, you become a part of that, and you realise that you can do things with that sort of knowledge. Nowadays, in general, there is a lot more space for that, partly because of the way music is made, and because it is something to be taken from samples. The same people who have completely based it on samples and a few beats are now coming back to reinventing, recreating a lot of those things themselves. People have looked a lot further, and have realised that you can go and put some jazz with it. There is a lot more colour and flavour, and world music plays a much bigger part in music today.

I don't want to change the way I live and I'm not successful in that way of people chasing me in the street. I've never wanted to make myself feel uncomfortable about going out looking however, doing whatever, when it's just this weird thing when if people recognise you – do I look like Neneh Cherry should look? I love what I do and it was really a big surprise and things have happened much faster than any of us ever thought they would.

When we were working on ['Raw Like Sushi'] Tim Simenon approached us with this 'Buffalo Stance' song which we've done before with Nellee Hooper, the Soul II Soul producer. 'Buffalo Stance' came out first, the album wasn't even finished and we just had a really good laugh and just did it over a couple of days. It was really spontaneous and it happened really quickly and it was really good because it summed up so many different aspects of what we were doing already but it was more digestible in a way. It was just a really good introduction but from there on it just kind of went – and there were no real intentions behind making the record except making the record.

At the time it was really exciting, a lot of fun. But after the first campaign I didn't really feel like going back out and throwing myself directly into making another album and being out there. You lose a certain amount of momentum in the public eye if you don't hit back really quickly but I think that you gain a certain amount of longevity if you take your time. I want to take my time with every record but I don't need to chill for three years between every album. It was just that so much had happened. I don't feel like packing it in, I don't feel like overdoing it.

I worked on the 'Red Hot and Blue' project which was a really important thing for me to do. My team, as such, went off and did the Massive Attack album. It was great to actually be a bystander and it was really inspiring. And I think a lot of that is reflected in the second album ['Homebrew']. I didn't really want to stick on another bloody mini skirt and jump up and down. I just didn't feel like it was what the world needed at that particular point in my career; I'd already done that.

I pushed a lot of the immediate pressures to the side because I felt that they didn't really have anything to do with why I and the people I was working with were doing what we were doing. I didn't really want to begin to take that into consideration – to actually make a big thing out of it. I've always been lucky to work with people who have been doing it because it's a way of life, and had a kind of commitment to what we've done. That was my mainstay and I tried to keep the whole thing within reason. It was like, this doesn't change me and who I am; it doesn't give me more reason to get up and think that I can get away with more things. So I had all these little alarm bells going off within me that were kind of urging me to really hold on to what I was doing.

When we started up Cherry Bear we became closer to the people that we worked with as a unit; you just realise that you need to keep things sane and I think that things are less likely to really change when you're with people that know what you're on about, that are in tune with the project. Because all of a sudden there are a hell of a lot of people who want to talk to you, who didn't want to talk to you before.

———————————————■———————————————

Around the first album, because obviously I was pregnant when I was promoting the early part of it, a lot of people saw it as being kind of revolutionary, whilst to me really it was a necessity. I had always felt unaffected by my own womanhood, I have never felt like I have got to stand up and really make myself clear; if I feel like shaking my arse, and pulling my skirt up and tucking it into my knickers I am going to do it! But all of a sudden, I think from going to meetings in record companies, there was a sort of question mark over me: 'How is your sexuality going to be presented? Is it going to be womanly and packaged like a Whitney Houston, or is it going to be wild and luscious?' Actually being pregnant at the time kicks a lot of that to the wind, and it wasn't like making an issue out of it. It diffused it. It just made me feel quite cocky, protected.

It did freak me out when I found out that I was pregnant, because I just thought, 'Oh my God, it wasn't planned'. I went to two abortion consultations but I couldn't bring myself to do it. It felt just like it was meant to be, for me, at that point. I had all those things in my head, like, 'Can I do this?' but at the same time, I had the support from other people around me, and there was this air in everyone who knew me, that it would be fine. I was quite hard on myself at times but I had this determination. I didn't let myself be tired; that is very like what I call the 'mother nature', the real woman, I am not going to let anyone see that I am really knackered, and I'm kind of insecure here, and that I'm a bit worried, and that I'm going to be OK. That is how you get through things, and you just do it. I think that it is in there, I think that a lot of this is actually conditioning, that comes from a long long way back. You know, it's like, 'I'm not going to complain', 'I'm going to be a good girl, I can deal with this', and it's OK, you are supposedly being your own best friend, but you are not because when you need something, you don't know how to ask for it.

For some reason [a baby] was just really what I needed at that particular point in my life, and there was no way I was going to pack everything in, and just be a mum, because I would have been useless. I think you have to be hard, you have to be really disciplined because kids are really greedy, and they need you, and you become so possessed by what they need, that I think it is really easy to give yourself up. Also, kids are people, and I really think that you are like their personal manager, managing them to be the best that they can be with your help. They have got a great kind of sense of needing to be independent. I have been lucky because I have got really good kids, but I never felt that I couldn't bring my kids with me. There was a space where I could give them what they needed, they could give me what I needed, where I could work, and they could be all right without me being there the whole time.

My mother gave up much more of her own creativity to be there for us, and I think that was partly to do with the way her and my stepfather decided that they wanted to have the family. My mother worked with my dad, they were a team, but a lot of her work became part of his work, and we were there all the time, and she was kind of alone I think, in mothering us, and running a big house. The people that came and stayed around us as a family, my friends, my dad's friends, other musicians, everyone was very into being 'free in themselves'. She would cook for twenty people and then she would have to do the dishes, and she still did amazing work, but I think she was too tired a lot of the time, to really give to herself. We moved, we travelled, but there was always a home there, and from that, I knew that I could take my kids with me, get on a plane, and have them backstage for the gig sometimes, and that they would like it, whereas if they had to go through it all the time, they wouldn't want it. I know a lot more women now, and families, are living like that. They can do that and feel like it's OK to be out there and to be a full person.

The working mother, is that a new concept? You must be bloody kidding me! Through the ages women have for a lot of the time been the mainstay of the family. It's just that it's a myth, the whole thing of the non-working mother, because women have had to have two jobs, the house, the home, the kids, and another job. But no credit has really been given.

We had an album cover ['Homebrew'] which was me holding an empty pram, and I think that from that album, it was like throwing away a bit of the 'mother nature' syndrome. I think around the first album it was a lot more blatantly aggravated, the energy from one record to another, we worked through transition, I very much went through a transition myself, where I grew and I gained a kind of confidence, because I felt like I didn't want to just re-perform what I had done before, I wanted to actually move on, and that's what we did.

I've grown up being influenced by a lot of things and I *am* a lot of things – a bit of a hip-hop chick, a bit of a punk rocker and I put all those things together when we created an image. It was just finding the right way to get that to shine through and finding the right details, the right trinkets; the energy was very much a street-based thing. A lot of people related to it and found that they could identify with it.

I think that it's dangerous if you start presenting yourself as a role model. If you are in the public eye, people that see you in that light are going to be influenced by that. I've got role models, I've got women and men that inspire me. It's great to be excited by someone, something, and inspired. But if you put too much on someone it can be really disappointing, because any person has faults and flaws. You can love someone and think what they do is great, and have them as a sort of inspiration, but I think that you can't model yourself on another person.

I've always felt that responsibility. You have to be aware of the fact that people look at what you do and I have always tried to say openly that each person has their own time to do things. If I want to give anything to young women and young men, it's that I would like to give them a sense that it's OK to be what you are and hopefully inspire that person to have self-confidence and get some sort of inner strength from it or just positivity, but think you can't do things in a way that another person has done them. I have always been really wary to say that it was great to leave school at fourteen and have kids at eighteen or whatever, because that's just how things happened with me, and I dealt with that and it was good for me.

There is that kind of transplanting, that it is just the scariest and the most exciting thing when you begin working with someone whose work you really respect. I think that it is like a way of re-birthing because you are very much what you are when you collaborate, but you find this weird little area in the middle. When we did 'Trout', Michael [Stipe] came more into our camp than we went into his camp, but he was very much part of making that song. It's very healthy to do that, because you go to areas and something happens which doesn't happen when you just work with people that you know. To mix and match is what the grounds of music that I make is about. It is about contradictions.

I think that it is important to be playful in your political correctness, and to make it human, because I think that political correctness is very much a thing of our time, and it is a fashion and it can be very shallow. It can become 'oh yeah, well, you know I recycle'. I haven't got the right to shove anything down anyone's throat, stand up and preach to anything or anybody, but I feel that it is really important to inject a certain amount of what I do with some kind of consciousness. You hear things that mean something to you, even in a song like 'Trout' which has got a clear message. People pick up on different things, and that isn't just saying things like you've got to have sex education, it is also saying, 'yeah, I want to have sex!' Which is why you need sex education.

It can become too righteous, and it can become incredibly boring. There has got to be an even balance, and I think that as long as you can project where you are coming from and what you feel without going on about it. People are intelligent, and you shouldn't underestimate people's intelligence. I think you have just got to be a bit aware, a bit conscious of what you think and what you mean, and just inject it cleverly in the right places where it is needed. Hiding, insinuating is more interesting in a way, because then you can make your own mind up, and that's a great thing about songs and lyrics, that you can get your own messages out of things.

There is an incredible amount of stigma around HIV and AIDS. We have come much much further on down the line now, people understand it better, but there was a phenomenal amount of tabooism and it was very segregated, and there was a lot of racism. I feel like, it's great to put out records but sometimes you have to do something. Also if you have got any media space which you can use, there are a lot of people out there that are interested in what you've got to say. I mean, me and my friends know what we think, but there might be a few young women out there who buy my records, who listen to what I say. The 'Red Hot and Blue' project came out at a time when there was nothing, no one was saying anything, really.

———————————————— ■ ————————————————

I have never lived in a place where I was racially abused constantly, but I have grown up being very aware of, being conscious of the fact that I am different. My mother's white but I was always aware of the fact that I was black. I have never felt ashamed of it, but I've always been aware of it. Growing up in Sweden, when I was a kid, my mother left me outside the post-office once when I was in a pram, three months old. She came out and there was a woman looking in, and she said, 'What do they eat?' My mother said, 'Bananas of course!' and rolled down the road. At school, they would read us these weird old-fashioned stories, '. . . and then they arrived on the island, and there was a line of Negro children holding hands . . .' Everyone in the class would look at me, and there was always that thing, where if you had an argument with someone, they would turn around and immediately you were a 'nigger'. If you drove a shopping trolley by mistake into an old lady in a store, she might turn around to you and say, 'Why don't you go back to where you came from?' It made me quite tough and it made me quite hard and that's definitely where I began to build my protection.

I grew up in New York as well, and I would make a point out of being black, absorb myself in black culture, and it was a great relief, I was just one of many. I think that also gave me a lot of self-respect. I had my father who's African, I went to Africa when I was fifteen, my stepfather who was a very proud black. I think I have got resilience from being brought up like that. Sometimes women get treated like that. Women are a different kind of like 'nigger' in a way. I think that having that, sometimes you could say you've got other things against you being black and a woman. That can be like double trouble! I think I have used a lot of the same mechanics that I used to protect myself against racism when I was growing up, later on in life getting through as a female.

My father did the biggest thing for me by taking me to Africa. I fought and I kicked, I didn't want to go, I wanted to stay in New York, I was going to CBGB's. I wanted to be in New York, because that was my world. I arrived in Nigeria wearing this camouflage Clash T-shirt, and within a week, I was honoured, privileged to be part-African. I didn't know what I thought Africa was like, I'd studied African dance and culture but I just didn't think that it existed as strongly as it did. I just thought it would be watered down somehow. Africa just gave me myself. I had never really thought about what being a woman was about, and all of a sudden, I was 'Wow, I'm a woman!' It was the strength and beauty of the women, the physicalness, the way they were with each other, they'd run the community, they'd run the market-place and they'd carry their kids with them.

You'd see people that you recognised, you would see gestures in people that you knew back in the States and think, 'God, that looks like . . .' It's like everyone has a grain of the beginning of time within them, something that has always been there and I could hear that race memory and feel it within myself. I still have the feeling of security that I got from going there.

I went back once, when Naima was three and a half. It was tough on her because she was very different to the other kids, and she had a temperament that none of the other kids had; she threw tantrums! When she came back she went into deep culture shock. It was very moving to see in a child, how weird it was to come back to where we are.

I have got a pattern of writing, where I'll start somewhere, and by the time I get to the end of the song the plot will have revealed itself. There is definitely a form in the way that I write and that is that when I start, if I am writing to a musical idea, like a beat or whatever, then usually there's a few words and I will sing or I'll find a melody, and certain words will just kind of come into my head. Before I go any further I will need to kind of find out somehow what it's about, if I haven't got something that I directly want to write about, and then usually, I describe the situation whether it's about a personal relationship to someone, it describes how the person feels and what happens, and what they've done to each other and then the final conclusion is where you end up. The next stage would be to then explode that, develop that and spend more time, because the song always runs out three to four minutes later. And to really play with those ideas. I've got a few things that I want to write about, stories, fiction.

Even if you are singing 'I' and 'me' and 'you', it can move you sometimes to tears when you sing something like that, it's not really, it's just like passing something through your system. It's like playing a part in a movie, you're not taking from your own well. You're touching on something else really. I think that music is kind of like that. It's like something that passes through you in a way, like creative forces and energy. You have to discipline yourself to produce and if it's something that you live off, you have to be disciplined.

I think for me each album has a form in a way, even if you are doing songs that are very different, it's a thread and once you've started off you can tread through it. When I'm not in work mode, I don't really write that much. I read a lot, I'll take notes, I'll write down lyrics, sentences someone might say, write little blurbs but I won't write a whole song, in general. It's like a kind of switch off and I just absorb things, because there is never that much time in between work. There's never more than maybe three months, and then I really begin to miss it.

I think that I've been lucky in a sense, because I think that there has always been quite a lot of [media] people who have enjoyed what I do, who have been fairly positive about it. You prepare yourself for a certain amount of crap, because no one wants to write just good things about a person, and there is always a point where people get sick of just reading nice things about you!

———————————————————■———————————————————

I really think that I should go back to school at some point in my life, so I really want to study, and I think that sometimes with my kids, I can be a bit over the top. Learning is just the biggest thrill in the world. It's just the best buzz. You know, I think that it is really unfortunate that education is so formatted, sort of taking out the book and then you put it down on to paper and then write it into another book. I think that you have to learn how to use the system, because there is a system. You can be a rebel and be a total anarchist, but I think that really you parade through the system when you learn how it functions and how to use it to your best advantage. That's actually when you gain a kind of power.

It's no easy thing, having kids, and working and being a good mother and being good to yourself, gaining acceptance, I mean it's really bloody tough. You work to have the life that you want, and you work to do the work that you want to do. It ends up sometimes you feel like you haven't really got any time to just be, because you are struggling and fighting. I think that can be said for a lot of people. It's hard and it's great, but nobody ever said it was easy, and you know my dad always says to me, 'Just don't let them ever change you!' And that's always been the best piece of advice.

Moe Tucker

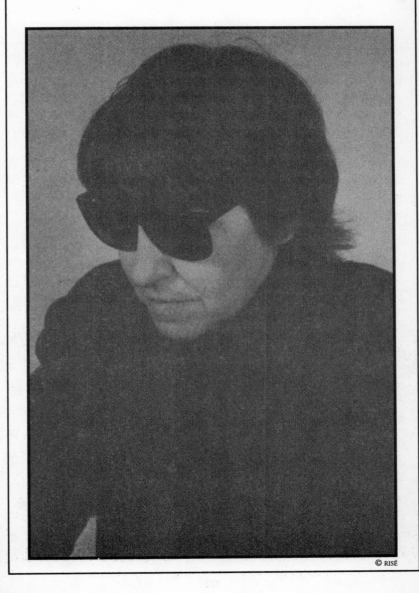

© RISÉ

M oe (Maureen) Tucker was born in New Jersey in 1945 and grew up in Long Island, New York. She taught herself to play drums, inspired by Rolling Stones and Bo Diddley records and the style of the Nigerian jazz drummer, Olatunji. In 1965, an introduction to co-founding Velvet Underground member Lou Reed – a friend of her brother's – led to her playing drums in the band, joining her friend, Sterling Morrison, John Cale and vocalist, Nico. Tucker developed an idiosyncratic drumming style – she preferred to stand at the drums, rather than sit, and turned the bass drum horizontal, hitting it with mallets. Her stripped-down kit and style of playing became a major part of the band's distinctive sound.

The pop-art protagonist, Andy Warhol, had 'adopted' The Velvet Underground and become the band's nominal manager. In 1966 The VU performed regularly at Cafe Bizarre, in Greenwich Village, New York City, and became the band-in-residence at Warhol's arts collective, The Factory. He integrated The Velvet Underground into his multi-media show, 'The Exploding Plastic Inevitable'. The same year, the band signed to MGM's Verve label.

In 1967 The Velvet Underground played a week-long series of concerts at the Montreal World Fair. Two months later, their debut album, 'The Velvet Underground and Nico', was released; it came to be regarded as a seminal and influential recording work. Produced – in name only – by Warhol, the album's distinctive features were Reed's amoral lyrical stance (including drug themes on 'Heroin') and Nico's melancholic vocal style. Nico left the band soon after and Warhol's relationship with them, too, began to wane.

The follow-up album, 'White Light, White Heat', was recorded in a single day in January 1968, at the end of a tour. Two months later, increasing tensions between Reed and Cale culminated in Cale leaving the band; he was replaced by Doug Yule. In 1969, 'The Velvet Underground' album was released, and the band signed to Atlantic Records after leaving Verve. In mid-1970, the band took up a residency in the New York City club, Max's Kansas City. Moe Tucker was pregnant with her first child, so Doug Yule's brother, Billy, deputised on drums. The album 'Loaded' was released; it included Reed's much-praised and later much-covered 'Sweet Jane'. Reed left The Velvet Underground soon after, to begin a solo career. Morrison left the following year, as did Moe Tucker, after a brief tour of Europe with the 'new' version of The Velvet Underground.

Moe Tucker moved to Phoenix, Arizona, with her family; apart from a two-week stint with a local band, she abandoned music in favour of childrearing, having five children in ten years. In 1982, she recorded her solo debut, an album of covers, 'Playing Possum', released on the Spy label. Four years later, her own material featured on her EP, 'MoeJadKateBarry'. Velvet Underground albums continued to trickle out – 'Live at Max's Kansas City' in 1972; the double album, '1969 – The Velvet Underground Live', in 1974; 'V.U.', a re-mix of old songs and some previously unreleased material, in 1985, edged close to the British Top Forty chart; and in 1986, the box-set 'Another View' was released.

Moe Tucker and her husband separated, and she moved her family to Douglas, Georgia. She did administrative work at the local Wal-mart chain store while writing new material for the album, 'Life in Exile After Abdication'. It was released in 1989, on the 50 Skidillion Watts label, financed by long-time fan, the magician Penn Jellette. The album featured guest appearances by Lou Reed and Sonic Youth; the sleeve notes were written by singer-songwriter and Modern Lovers frontman, Jonathan Richman.

In June 1990, Tucker, Cale, Reed and Morrison reunited in memory of Andy Warhol (who died in 1987) to perform 'Heroin', at the opening of a retrospective of his work, held by the Cartier Foundation, near Paris. It was the first time they had played together since 1969. On Moe Tucker's 1991 album, 'I Spent a Week there the Other Night', the three ex-Velvets also played on the track 'I'm Not'; Sterling Morrison joined her band, which toured to promote the album. In December of that year, Imaginary Records released a five-album boxed set, 'The Imaginary Box' of VU material, including an album of cover versions by various artists.

By 1993, relations between Reed, Cale and Morrison had improved so dramatically that they announced plans to re-form the band for a tour of Europe. In June, almost three years to the day since their brief reunion at the Warhol retrospective, the band played at Wembley Arena in London on the first leg of their tour. A live album, 'Live MCMXCIII', was released in late-1993.

Moe Tucker's fifth solo recording, 'Dogs Under Stress', was released on the New Rose label in early 1994; among the guest players was Sterling Morrison.

Moe Tucker lives in Douglas, Georgia.

I'd known Sterling since I was about twelve because he was my brother's friend. Sterling met Lou also through my brother, they became friends in college. They fooled around playing guitar; they had been playing together with John and Angus [MacLise] for a while. They got a job where they were going to be paid, and Angus didn't like that idea so he quit! So they were scrambling for a drummer at the very last minute, and Sterling said, 'Tucker's sister plays drums'. So Lou came to my house to see if I could actually keep time, and I passed the audition! It was just supposed to be for that one show, just three songs. From that show, they immediately got another job two nights later but they weren't allowed to play drums in there because it was too noisy. So they said, 'come and play the tambourine'. So, from there I was in the band.

I started playing drums because I really liked music, and I could learn it much quicker than guitar. All I had to do was buy a snare drum and that's just what I did. I was so nuts about The Rolling Stones and Bo Diddley that just sitting listening to it wasn't enough, I wanted to be doing something. I would sit in my room for hours and just listen and play along. At every moment, I was doing it for fun. I just lucked out, that the way I played worked perfectly with the kind of music the others were playing. We just all played the way we liked to, and sounded the way we wanted to. That group of four people which had different styles, and different likes, made a very different sound.

I consciously, purposely, didn't learn more about drums because I didn't want to sound like anybody else and I knew, once you learn to do a twelve-bar roll, it's very hard not to do it. Also I was trying to get an African sound, at first; I really liked African drumming. I noticed in records that I liked, what I liked about the drumming was that the person was just in the background, playing drums, keeping the tempo and not ever taking over the song. I like Charlie Watts, for instance; he's just there, he's perfect, he never overtakes a song, if he does a roll, it's heaven, it's perfect. I can't stand drum solos, I just hate them! I can't stand real fancy drummers who are thrashing around. It's so ridiculous. You don't see it so much any more but there was a period there, in the '70s, where in a video, for instance, the drummer would have literally twenty drums and thirty cymbals. Get real! It's rock and roll, what's going on? Of course, if you've got all that stuff, you've got to hit it! I hate that kind of drumming. And I don't like the sound of cymbals, so you'll very rarely hear cymbals on a Velvet song.

I wanted to have the bass drum up a certain way and the only way to play it was to turn it and stand up. And also I can't stand songs where all you hear is the bass drum throughout the whole song, it begins to drive me crazy! So, I don't like that foot thing all the time, so I didn't miss that and I wanted to have the deepness of the bass drum available for banging.

With the Velvets, when we first played, we used to do a lot of improvising: thirty minutes, forty minutes, or just two minutes, whatever anybody felt like. I always felt that my job was to keep something going that everybody could come back to. I would be keeping one beat and John would go off and do something totally nuts that had nothing to do with the beat; Lou would be doing something crazy! To me, I was the rhythm section and there had to be something to go back to, and for the audience to hold on to: 'This *is* a song, there's the beat!'

We never tried to be phoney or different in any way. I would feel so uncomfortable; even now, posing for a picture I'm embarrassed. I feel like a fool! My American label was talking about doing a video and I thought, 'Oh God, I hope they don't want me to act because I can't do that!' If Lou or John or Sterling ever said, 'OK, we're going to all get suits, we're all going to jump up and down on stage and on the last beat of "Heroin" we'll all fall to the floor!' I'd have had to say, 'No way, guys, get another drummer!' But they weren't into that either, any kind of antics or doing any kind of act.

I was always proud of the fact that we didn't put on airs of any kind – clothing, or stage presence – we just played our music. We couldn't sell records to save our lives. Also, we weren't – and this sounds saintly – but we weren't in it to make a hit record. If no one had ever heard of us, I'd have still felt it was worth it because I think it was incredible music. We really liked and were proud of the music we played and that was enough for us: 'Wow, that sounded great! That's what we're here for!'

Andy [Warhol] was just a really nice guy, I liked him a lot. It's hard to explain, because when I start to explain how I felt about it, it sounds like I'm a little saint but the fact is that I was this jerk from Long Island and The Factory was just so much fun to me. I just loved it there. Nobody ever tried to make me take drugs or made fun of me because I didn't; it wasn't like that at all. At that time I was extremely shy and completely lacking in confidence in any field, and it would have been the prime territory for me to be made to feel like I was the biggest jackass, but I had the total opposite reaction.

I liked Nico, but we were never big friends because she was from a completely different world. She was this incredibly beautiful person, and I was this schlump! I liked her and I found out later, very happily so, that she liked me too. In 1982 I was playing with a band in Phoenix where I lived, and we went to California to play a show, the one and only show we ever played. And Nico was right down the street. I hadn't seen her at that point, for ten or twelve years. So I thought, 'I'll just say hello'. And she was so happy to see me. After her show, and my show, we went back to the hotel, and we sat around drinking beer and talking. It was so nice; I'm really glad that happened.

You never knew who'd walk in to The Factory. What was fun about it all was that those people were funny as hell. They were all very, very well-read, very well-spoken and just telling you the story of how they poured their Coke and spilled it, you'd be laughing because of the English they'd use! It was crazy but fun-crazy. It was not mayhem or lunacy or horrible things going on. Andy was, at the time, the hot ticket to get at your party, so every person in New York would invite Andy, no matter what it was, a coming-out party or whatever! If you invited Andy, you got thirteen freaks because he didn't go alone. If he was going to a party, we'd just go. That was part of the charm, people wanted him there because he was so different. We went to a party in the Dakota [apartment building] which now that I'm a grown-up I think yeah, that's nice but I've seen fancier things, but back then . . . there we were, me and Sterling from Levittown, with these people who wouldn't spit on you in the street, and you had absolutely nothing in common with them. They wanted you there so they could tell their friends the next day. So it was kind of, 'What the hell, come on in and drink some champagne!' Sterling has very good memories, Lou and John have very good memories of that time. Good memories of a lot of fun, because of the people who were around.

It was always a thrill to me to be on stage. I suppose if I was a guy I would have felt overshadowed but I don't have that male ego problem. I thought they were quite stunning, I wasn't jealous or angry, I was glad I was playing with them. Maybe if we'd been doing it for ten years, I'd have thought, 'I don't have a house! I don't have shoes!' Maybe I would have started getting bitchy about it. We were never on a quest to get rich so it never occurred to me that we should change. I was just having fun. And really loved and was proud of the music. I'm so glad that we didn't ever sell-out, I hate to use that word! We didn't ever say, 'Lou, write a damn rock song and let's all get rich.' That's not what we were interested in. We just played what we liked and when we got tired of each other, or whatever the reason was, we stopped playing.

I thought, 'We're just playing this great music, what's the problem?' I just didn't understand it, I still don't understand it. If there's someone you just didn't like, who really irritated you, who was always spitting on you, it's different; but when you like them and you respect their music, what's the problem? [After Cale and Reed left] I was trying to make it work but at that point, it was just a band. It was more fun to go play in Boston than get a job in a local office so I hung around for a while. Then when Sterling left we had already booked a tour in Europe. I didn't want to go; there was me and these three guys. Signs were put up saying 'The Velvet Underground' and that pissed me off. I went for two reasons: I always wanted to go to Europe so that was a dream come true, and I really felt 'What a rip-off to have in the papers "The Velvet Underground", it's four people they never saw before!' That was lousy too because who-ever had bought tickets, bought tickets with The Velvet Underground name and there wouldn't have been one Velvet even there.

It never occurred to me to have music as my career, which is why I just went home when we disbanded. I had my daughter so I had to start thinking, 'I have to have a paycheck every week.' I didn't stop playing music begrudgingly, it was just feeling, 'I don't like this, it's not fun any more; it's not anything to be proud of.' It wasn't anywhere near what the Velvet feeling was. So it was very easy to walk away from that. I had four more babies; I was just a housewife. There was no time to be pining for a different career. I had five kids all under ten years old and that takes a lot of time. Even if you don't do a good job, it takes a lot of time! I couldn't even consider going on a tour with so many little kids. It just didn't occur to me.

It is my career now, just by luck and chance really; I just thought, 'What the hell, I'll try it! It'll be fun to make a record!' It's worked out fine, so that I can support my family on Velvet royalties and what I earn. Penn [Jellette] is a big, big Velvets fan and always has been, and his idea was to have a little label that he would put up the money for, so that people he liked would have the chance to make a record. That's how I made the second record. The first one, I made in my living-room! It never, ever occurred to me to try to write a song. I would just sing. When Andy died I was watching the news about him dying, and I just got this little message of these two lines, 'Lost an old friend today, And I feel so far away' and I wrote it down. A couple of days later I sat down, not even with the idea of a song, and I wrote it. I really like that song ['Andy'] a lot. That was the first thing I ever wrote.

The first four or five songs I wrote were all about things I was really happy about or mad about: Andy dying, working at the damn Wal-mart. I find myself admiring people who can shoot out these throwaway songs because I can't do that yet. If I'm going to write a song, I can't think of what to say, unless it means something to me. I don't mean I'm Shakespeare or something! It's a failing on my part; to write about something you never do, like surfing, I can't do that. I wish I could because I could fill up the albums quicker! When I first started to try to write songs, I listened much more closely to lyrics on the radio or MTV. And I was amazed: 'What's that supposed to mean? He's saying the same thing over again fifteen times!'

When I first was writing, I wrote 'Andy', 'Hey, Mersh' and 'Work'. As I finished each one, I'd look at it and think, 'Does this sound stupid?' I had a little recorder and I made a tape of me playing guitar and singing these three songs and I sent it to

Lou. And he loved them; he called me and said, 'These songs are great! I didn't know you could write songs!' That was a big boon to me because I really admire his song-writing, and for him to think the lyrics were not just stupid meant a lot to me. You can't judge yourself. Then I started listening to the radio and I thought, 'My song isn't stupid, it's pretty good!'

I'd feel stupid singing 'oh baby, don't go, I'll die if you leave me', because I'm not thinking that kind of thing. I couldn't write it because I've never felt like that about anyone. So luckily, the kind of songs I wound up writing were like 'Spam Again'. When I was writing it, I didn't think, 'oh, everyone will feel this way', it's just how I felt. A lot of people have said, 'I love your music, I can identify with the lyrics, it's just like at home!' Every song doesn't have to have a big, deep meaning. In fact, when [Bob] Dylan first became popular, when he was still folkie, I couldn't stand him because I felt he was preaching. I thought, 'I don't need this creep to tell me how to live or who to like, I know what I'm doing!' It just irritated me. What I liked at the time, and still love, is 'Doo Ron Ron' and 'My Boyfriend's Back'; it's the music and the melody to those songs, it's not the lyrics. If I could write a song like one of those I would be really happy. I wish I could just whip out a little 'Maybelline' or 'Johnny B. Goode', these great songs that don't really mean something sincere to anybody, they're just great rock and roll songs.

When [The Velvets] recorded, we wanted to record something we could reproduce on stage, not do fifty-nine overdubs so that when you go to play, it doesn't even sound like the record. That was something we always had in mind. And that's what I wanted with my records. I was worried about me being the focal point and me being the singer. I thought, 'Oh, God, I know I'm a lousy singer!', but it seems to be OK. I'm not trying to be something I'm not. That's the way I sing. I do the best I can. I don't have a pretty voice, I very often miss a note!

When I play, too, with my band, in each song there's two notes that one out of ten times I'll actually hit! I always try, but you never know . . . and when I do, I'll stop and say, 'Let's do it again!' and the audience love that. Maybe I'll hit it again, maybe I won't. Or if I miss it I'll say, 'Let me try again!' One night we tried four times! There are a lot of people who are sick and tired of Guns N'Roses and Madonna, and all that stuff, the thousands of dancers, the costumes; to me that's not rock and roll, that's a Broadway show. There are a lot of young people who are not attracted by that, they want to see a band playing rock and roll and having fun. To me, that's the key: to have fun. If you're not having fun on stage, why would the audience have fun? So, my shows are very casual.

When I first told Sterling I was going to do a tour he was stunned. On the phone, I could practically hear him faint: 'What are you going to do? What are you going to sing?' He was amazed that I would try this. I said, 'I'm going to sing the songs I wrote, and some covers.' When I went on my first tour, I was very worried. I knew we'd get lots of people because here's this ex-Velvet that no one's ever seen, and people want to come and that's great. Hopefully, they would go away liking my music. But I thought, if the audience is full of fifty-year-old ex-Velvet fans, I guess this will be my first and only tour, because I don't want that! I figured there's going to be some goof-balls out there yelling for 'Heroin' like there always is. I was amazed; there were sixteen- and seventeen-year-old kids; it was a young audience and they loved it. They loved it in a whole different way than I loved Bo Diddley, for instance. I could faint when I hear Bo Diddley play, and they're not fainting at *my* singing or guitar-playing, that's for sure! It's the whole persona, they know this is no bullshit, 'Here's Moe and she's singing this song, it's not the best voice I ever heard but what the hell! She's having fun and so will I!'

When I first started getting back into music the very first tour I did, about five years ago, was six weeks long. I realised that's too long; it's too long for my children, it's too long for my mother who was watching them, it's a little too long for me. So I never go away for more than five weeks. That was a good lesson and I learned it right away. So I always keep things down to four or five weeks. What's hard about it is just that I'm their mother, and that's who they want there. They know what they can do and what they can't do. Whereas when my mother comes over, it's a whole different set of rules. In this way, it's easier when they're young, they just accept that but when they get a little older, they say [things like] 'Mom would let me go to the video store, why can't I?' And Grandma says 'no you can't go', trying to be protective and careful with them because she feels very responsible. As they get older, it's more difficult, for them and for me. When I'm away, it's always in my mind that they're home. If it wasn't for my mother, I could not have started all this. She comes over and stays at my house and does everything, and does it absolutely willingly.

———————————————— ■ ————————————————

When you go through something like being in The Velvet Underground with someone, that's a life-long thing. Like if you're on a championship football team with this group of people, it's something special; if you were astronauts and went to the moon with these three guys, you had something special, that nobody else can get into. So I had that female sentimentality of wanting to hold things together; I love them all dearly.

For the album ['I Spent a Week There The Other Night'], John had said, 'I'll play on it if you want me' and Lou had said that, and there was one song ['I'm Not'] I was thinking I want us all to play on, it has all the elements that they each do that I love. Lou played on one other, John played on one or two others and Sterling played on most of them. That worked out well. John came into the studio the very last day I was there and he came in with his twenty thousand dollar viola, saying, 'What do you want me to play?' It was great!

A big part of it was that everybody grew up a little. Lou had done some work with me, and he'd done some work with John, and Sterling was playing with me. At the Cartier [Foundation] thing, Sterling and Lou got to make up after twenty years of not speaking. We just had the greatest time. I think it was the best four days I've ever had in my life! The four of us, together, which we hadn't been in twenty years. They got to see how much they really liked each other, not just John and Sterling, but all three of them. They just shook hands and said, 'How are you doing?', and that was the end of it, after twenty years of bullshit! So that was a big part of us even being able to sit down together.

We had a bet going about the average age of our audience and what their reaction would be. They all said, 'It's going to be all of these fifty year olds.' I said, 'You're crazy, it's going to be all kids!' They said, 'These people, they're going to be there to see us fail, they'll be glad to see us fail.' I said, 'Bullshit! Who's going to pay thirty dollars to see someone fail?' I won all the bets – they never paid me! The whole reason for [their attitude] was a protection, because if we did fail, they could say, 'We knew that would happen!' But I knew that none of us would have done it if we thought we'd fail. I wouldn't have risked our reputation for anything. But I suppose I was the only one who had the nerve – and being the woman, and not worrying about the ego – to say, 'We're going to be great!' At one show, we were in the eating area before the show and we were looking down into the parking lot and we saw all of these kids, fifteen years old. When you play in big places, you don't see anybody, you don't know how old anybody is. At my shows, we stay on stage and sell T-shirts or sign autographs, so you see everybody. So I knew who was coming to my shows, and I knew who was coming to Lou's shows. I said, 'We have a new generation here, boys!'

I had played with my band in Czechoslovakia about a year before the [reunion] tour and Vaclav Havel came to my show; he sat right down at the front. It's one thing to say, 'I really love your music', but it's another to come out to a dump and listen, when you're the president. He stayed for the whole thing and came backstage after the show. He was trying to convey to me what our music had meant to him. I was totally overwhelmed. Those people went to jail because of rock and roll. He seems to be a genuine man, a really good man. To see someone who, twenty-five years ago, was creeping around listening to our stuff

and loving it, is just overwhelming. I don't know if I would play
Bo Diddley if I thought I was going to go to jail for it! To see
him become not only a respected author but the president of a
country is really something.

———————————————◼———————————————

I never had any problem. I was just playing drums, it wasn't a
campaign or a statement, I just liked playing drums and why
shouldn't I? I don't ever remember anyone either in the band or
in the audience saying, 'Why are you playing drums? You're a
girl!' Maybe half of them didn't know I was a girl! I don't feel
like a pioneer or a campaigner because I didn't have to fight to
get into the group. They liked how I played drums, that's all.
When I was younger it was the girls who bought the records,
they were buying Fabian and all that. Now I think it's either
even or turned around, where it's guys buying records. Yet you
never saw a girl playing anything; she was always the singer,
maybe playing a piano or keyboards. That's always been a mystery, I could never figure that out.

We'd play places where there'd be four other bands and I'd
be the only woman backstage. I didn't think, 'Why aren't there
any girls back here? There are twenty guys and no girls.' It didn't
strike me as odd then but nowadays it would. I really like
Chrissie Hynde a lot. I like the fact that she plays guitar and
looks so comfortable with her guitar. It's nice to see a woman
have some fun with the music you've been buying all your life.

Now, there's a thousand times more women musicians
than when I was around, but even so, there's very few women
music *players*. When you think of every culture, when you see a
documentary, for instance, on Africa, it's always the men playing the drums and the women dancing. Dancing requires
rhythm so why can't they play the drums?

Evelyn Glennie

© MARK MARNIE

E velyn Glennie was born in Aberdeen, Scotland, in 1965. From the age of twelve, she studied timpani and percussion. By this time, she had become profoundly deaf. In 1982, she entered the Royal Academy of Music in London and proceeded to win a clutch of awards, among them the Gold medal in the Shell/LSO Music scholarship in 1984. Two years later, she travelled to Japan to further her studies after being awarded the Munster Trust scholarship. By now, she had honed her 'listening' skills – she 'hears' the music through vibrations, often performing barefoot, by studying the scores rather than listening to the material, and by observing the movements of those on stage with her, from the conductor to the other players.

She performed Bartok's 'Sonata for Two Pianos and Percussion', with Sir Georg Solti and Murray Perahia, in a documentary for the American CBS network. The subsequent recording won a Grammy award in 1989. Her debut performance at the BBC Proms – the annual Promenade Concerts at the Royal Albert Hall in London – in 1989, featured the first ever solo percussion recital at the Proms, and three years later, she was invited back to give the première of the specially commissioned concerto by James MacMillan, 'Veni, Veni Emmanuel', which she later recorded. Her other solo recordings include 'Rebounds', 'Rhythm Song', 'Dancin'' and 'Light in Darkness'.

In 1990 Evelyn Glennie was voted Scots Woman of the Decade, the same year her autobiography, *Good Vibrations*, was published in Britain. In 1991 she won the Royal Philharmonic

113

Hymn to Her

Society's Heidsieck Soloist of the Year award. She is a Fellow of the Royal College of Music and the Royal Academy of Music and has been awarded honorary doctorates at both Aberdeen and Warwick Universities.

Glennie has developed a wide interest in 'world' music, including forays into Korean percussion (filmed for a BBC documentary), and Brazilian percussion, with a trip to the Rio carnival (filmed for ITV's 'South Bank Show'). She has made dozens of television appearances, and presented the BBC's 'Soundbites' music series. Two major documentaries have been made about her life (by the BBC and Yorkshire Television). In an effort to encourage wider recognition for, and experimentation in percussion repertoire, she founded the Evelyn Glennie Percussion Composition award, which is open to all UK composers.

Evelyn Glennie is acknowledged as the first full-time solo percussionist in the world. In 1993 she was awarded an OBE. The same year, she joined the music advisory panel of the Arts Council of Great Britain, but resigned several months later, in protest at the Council's decision to cut funding of two of London's major orchestras. The Council later rescinded its decision.

She lives in Cambridgeshire with her husband, Greg Malcangi, a musician and recording engineer.

I was probably lucky in that I lost my hearing as a child, in which case, the development stage is still happening, whereas if I'd lost my hearing when I was fourteen or fifteen, that's a very dangerous time and likewise if you're older, you can't adjust in the same way and so everything is affected. But as a child, if you fall off your bike you get up again and you get on it and you start riding. It's the same when you lose some faculty or other, then everything else compensates, everything else is razor-sharp and the word 'problem' doesn't arise – it only comes from other people's lips.

A lot of people have said to me, 'Well, you just haven't said

114

anything about your deafness in your book [*Good Vibrations*].'
And, basically, that's because there's nothing to say! This is how
it was. It was just something that was accepted, not just by me
but by my family. There wasn't any crisis or anything. My parents just aren't like that, so there wasn't anything to make a
mountain out of, really. It was very straightforward and I think
this helped, whereas if they had suddenly come around and said
'Oh, my God, we've got a deaf child', things may have been a
lot different. Likewise, my brothers, they just accepted it and
they made the necessary adjustments as well and that's that.

I'm probably the sort of person that eventually finds some
positive way; I can't tell you how, it's just the way it is, and you
somehow get over it. And I think a lot of it has to do with the
people you are surrounded by. So I had great friends who were
very supportive and had an awful lot of humour. This helped
me a lot.

The strange thing about it was that I hadn't intended becoming
a musician as such and I think that allowed the pressure to be
completely laid off. Because I just auditioned for the [Royal]
College and the [Royal] Academy, just for experience, to see
what it was like. And I had no idea that the places would be
open. Then suddenly people came into my life, people who
really believed in what I wanted to do. The Rachlins [composer,
Ezra, and his wife, Ann, founder of the Beethoven Fund for
Deaf Children] at first thought, when they heard me play the
piano, 'I'm not so sure you should go in for this kind of thing.'
Then I explained, 'Look, I'm not a pianist and I don't want to
be a pianist, but listen to this percussion-playing and see what
you think.' And so, once they turned around and said 'yes, go
for it', this was the necessary medicine I needed, this was the real
encouragement that I desperately needed at that stage.

Also there was a feeling where I could remember the summer before I went to the Academy, I just thought to myself, 'I'm
really, really going to have to work so hard at this place, because

I'm going to be the worst student there.' I really didn't believe that my standard of playing was suitable to get to London; I just thought it was a totally different world. So I was prepared to have to work, I was prepared to be bottom of the class at all times, and so it was that kind of mentality where I knew I'd have to work, and I had my aims clearly set out and it saved an awful lot of time in the long run. And I knew in my first year as a student, that I would only stay three years there, I had no inclination to stay a fourth. In year one, I planned to just concentrate on the mechanics of playing, get my technique sorted out, settle down to being a student, learn repertoire and so on, and just cope with activities within the Academy. I didn't want any media attention or anything like that, which of course was happening then. So, it was just a time when I could develop myself. In the second year, for some reason, I grew a bit home-sick. I found it a really tough year, where I found lots of things difficult within the course. It seemed an awfully long year. I was thinking about home an awful lot and I was missing home. I was longing for it. Also in that year there was the Shell-LSO competition and so that was something to work for; that was probably one of the main aims. But, again, I took that so lightly because I had no feeling that I would get anywhere in it, so again, the pressure wasn't there. And maybe that was the trick! Then the third year was the year when I was preparing to leave, so I was creating concert programmes and really developing as a musician.

As far as the [Academy's] instrumentalists, not the percussionists, there was no problem at all. There was a problem with the percussion set-up but that wasn't so much the media attention [I was getting], that was because I wasn't part of the system. They all wanted to be orchestral players, that was what their teacher was, that was what was expected of them and then suddenly, for someone to arrive who was delving into the concertos, the solo repertoire, who wanted to be a soloist, this was totally alien to them. Why did I have the right to say that I could be a soloist? They were using the word 'soloist' as an individual being better than the others, it wasn't that at all. It was just because I went in there thinking, 'God, they're all going to be miles ahead of me', and that still isn't the reason why I'm doing solo work. There are loads of people out there who are a million times better, it isn't about that. It's about creating your own interpretation, creating your stamp-mark on the piece. It's not showing off, it's just that this is how I want to express the piece. I think that's very important, because I knew earlier on that my technique was fairly average, and I could improve and I knew what to do, but I think that's a very key point. I was in competition with myself, I desperately wanted to get better, I desperately wanted to learn the repertoire and I desperately wanted to be in control. I didn't care what the others were doing, that was up to them, if they found something that made them happy, that's great. Likewise, if I was really interested in being in an orchestra, I'd have gone to town in really trying to explore that area of music as being the best that I possibly could in that field. This is the interesting thing when you go over to the States, is that you find specialists on tambourine and they know the instruments inside out and the history, and everything else about it. And that gives me a lot of inspiration. You see marimba specialists, or drum-kit specialists, and you just realise where you are in comparison, so it always gives you the desire to work towards that.

I think [national] attitudes are different – certainly in the States, it's drilled into them that they're the best, that America is the best and that is probably good but I think it also has its negative points. But people in general over there are very technically-minded so what they do with their [drum-]sticks is absolutely amazing but the heart is somewhere else. Over in Europe, I would say that the heart really is there, the technique can sometimes be there and sometimes not. It is a very different attitude. I'm the sort of player where I like to think the heart is there, and the technique is somewhere there, but you're not really thinking about it. It's probably how I speak in a way, where my vocabulary is very small, my statements are disjointed and so on, so, to give a speech would be very, very difficult for me but nevertheless I can hopefully get across what I'm wanting to say through facial expression or movement or through eyes or something. It's the same with music, you can't put across what you want to say by just using the actions, you have to use your being.

Over the years I've realised in my library I have about two hundred percussion concertos. When I was a student at the Academy, they had three. Since that time, I've found over two hundred but many of them are not published so it's actually coming into contact with the music information centres and the composers themselves, to find those pieces. So there's a lot out there, it's just getting your hands on it. But of course I hadn't realised that at such a young age and I just got so frustrated at standing at the back, just waiting and waiting and waiting and then being dictated to, about how to play the piece, because the conductor dictates the tempo and so on. And I couldn't bear the fact of this happening, I wanted to be in control of the interpretation, I wanted to be in control of the programming for the concert. And most of all, I just wanted to play. And I've found that solo work really fulfilled all those things and more.

I just had to fulfil my musical needs. I had to be able to play what I wanted, I had to be in control of the audience. I wanted to give pleasure to the audience, I wanted to say, 'This is me playing here', and sometimes if I played an orchestral part, people wouldn't really notice you until you made a mistake, in which case the whole world came crashing down! You would walk on-stage, you would walk off-stage and you didn't really get to know your audience but of course since that time my perception and my years of orchestral playing have changed greatly and it *is* an art. Orchestral percussion really is an art. It's something that I appreciate now, but I still don't have any desire to become an orchestral player although I am now setting up my own ensemble. So I feel ready to play with a small group of musicians where each member is featured.

There wasn't a role model and so this was the dangerous

thing, I suppose. And the real challenge was that everything I did was an experiment, it was like walking on a tight-rope and sometimes you would fall and sometimes your balance was pretty good. And I think this was the main thing that scared a lot of people and they would say 'well just don't go for it', because they had no idea what would happen to me, so they were probably saying it out of the goodness of their hearts but I couldn't see it like that at the time. But of course now there are many people who do solo work but not on a full-time basis, so it's still difficult to have a real role model.

Certainly I wasn't thinking about [the problems] in the way that it's because I'm female. That never crossed my mind. And when I was a student, despite the fact that there were about ten lads playing percussion and then me, again it still didn't cross my mind that I was female. It's just that it wasn't part of the system; and you had to be part of the system to succeed. I would have rather got out of music than be forced into an area of music which I just knew wasn't right. Even now, I still say to myself, 'If I can't pursue a solo career . . .' and now, I'm branching out to other areas, such as composition and writing, if I can't do what feels right within myself, I'm just going to find something else completely. I'm not going to fight it as such.

EMI had approached me when I left the Academy; they were ready to record, but I certainly wasn't. The repertoire that was discussed at that stage was repertoire that would have been very nice but I just didn't want to play it; it just wasn't how I wanted to be represented. So we just left it. And then RCA came along and, by that time, I was more experienced as a player, because you have to have the performance experience. I really believe that; you must feel what it's like to be on a platform, to really perform, and so I had a much bigger repertoire to choose from and I felt ready to do it. So it's very important to have that control, certainly over the record company, otherwise you can be put in a position where you'll do it because they want you to do it. Certainly they can give you advice, and some of the things they say, I think 'I've never thought about that before, and I can see why you want to record this type of material', but you must feel at one with the pieces.

What attracts me to a piece is whether the style first of all is to my liking and I think that's probably the main thing that I think about. And how I can relate that to past experiences in playing music and then I think about the practicalities of playing it. Can I actually handle this piece mechanically, can I play it? All the time you're looking at it, you're conjuring ideas, really right from the word 'go'. Like really reading a book, you look at the title and you think of an idea, 'What is this book about? What does the title mean?' Then you read the back cover and you gain some more knowledge and some more ideas and you decide whether you want to buy it or not. So I'm basically looking at the title, looking at the style, looking then at the practicalities which would probably be equivalent to looking at the price of the book. The interpretation is like a lifetime thing, even if it's a piece you've played a million times, you just go on and on trying it in different ways and sometimes you may play it the same way for the next twenty performances and suddenly something happens and you want to try something different, something may become so different with it, actually on the platform, that you hadn't expected before. If it's concertos, then all the orchestras have conductors who will give you something different, so it changes.

I feel very uncomfortable if I have to stand up and play without saying a word. It just doesn't feel right to me and again, I've just basically followed my instincts, 'This is what I want to do and I'll do it.' And if it means just introducing things to the audience, just talking to the audience, and if it feels right, then why not do it? I feel that it's important, if people come along to my concerts, music is one part of the concert. They're seeing Evelyn Glennie, and they're not just seeing the musician side of Evelyn Glennie, they're meeting Evelyn Glennie. I know if I go to a concert, I want to meet the person, I want to really be introduced to that person, not just as a musician, I want to know what their voice is like, how they use their hands. I want to see them smile, I want to know how they communicate with us, and that's all part of the performance. It can also allow you to understand why they play as they do. Sometimes you come across a very shy, quietly-spoken person and then suddenly their performance is the complete opposite, and you think 'now, that's very interesting'. Or sometimes you may come across someone who is so energetic and active, but then when they come to play, they're quite the opposite. Again that's interesting: 'I wasn't expecting that!'

I'd made it quite clear that I did not want to be perceived as some kind of freak or other; that just isn't me. When I look back on it now, I think 'well, too much was concentrated on deafness', but at the time, it felt right. At the time, I felt I had to get this across, get it out of my system. So that now, we can really avoid it, in terms of it being just some sort of headline or other. Sometimes we're successful and sometimes not. Like in America, everything is hyped, and everything is blown out of all proportion. In this country . . . people know who I am and the music critics simply concentrate on the music. And they know it's foolish of them not to, and abroad, certainly in Europe and in Japan, they concentrate on the music. A lot of them don't know because it's not in the biography and I'm just another musician who's turned up to play and that's that. And those who do know will sometimes put it in and sometimes not. What does anger me is if I present a biography to concert promoters which doesn't mention about my deafness, and they put something in. That annoys me very much indeed because for me, it's as though you're saying, I have brown hair. It's personal and that's it really.

If people are encouraged that's great, but at the end of the day I'm just a normal musician. I try to get on with my work and that's it. I try to do the best I can and if people feel encouraged by that, then that's wonderful but it's not my job to stand up there and say, 'This is what you should fight for.' I'm just doing what feels right for me. I will only do that if I feel so strongly about [something] – for example, presenting music in schools for the deaf I feel strongly about, so I'm going to broadcast the fact that all people should experience music. But then, it's up to them how they treat it, how they want it to be a part of their lives. What I do get is 'Why isn't my Jimmy a great musician?' That sort of thing. I have a brother who's tone-deaf, what can I do about that? So, for some reason, people assume that because I'm a musician then their little boy or little girl should be able to play despite the fact that they're deaf. Of course that isn't the case, we're not all musical. I can't cook but that has nothing to do with my ears; I simply cannot cook! I'm not interested in cooking, I have no desire to learn how to cook. I can do the very basics out of necessity in order to live but it's just not in me.

———————————————■———————————————

I always believe that we must try as many things as possible, we must try to find positive things, and how they can affect our lives. If it means just enjoying music as a listener, or just playing an instrument because you love it, but not to any professional level . . . One of the things that I basically try to promote is for people to just experience music; that's all I'm asking them. Likewise, to give contemporary repertoire a chance. Go and listen to it, if it doesn't mean anything, it doesn't mean anything, but at least you'll know and you can talk from first-hand experience of the music. But to not really give that a chance or to not really give the time, or, maybe even have the opportunities to explore what you are good at, then that would be a shame. One of my brothers loves farming, and no matter what we do we just won't change that. He's found the thing in his life that makes him happy. Likewise, I've found the thing in my life that makes me happy. If I started to do something which didn't create good vibes within myself then I'd be an unhappy person; I wouldn't be like I am at the moment, I wouldn't be confident, I'd be frustrated probably, I'd be grumpy. I'd carry out a very mundane sort of life and everyone around me would be affected by that.

I think that we're so influenced by what we hear on the radio, and it's pop music. It's 4/4 time and it can become quite tedious so we have to make our own effort to experience other sorts of music and that can often be going in the car, and out and about to a concert hall or going into a record shop and taking the time to look at the rows and rows of recordings and different titles. It is nice if you can make the effort, to take something that you would never dream of listening to, go to a concert that you'd never think you would ever attend, so if it's something like a concert of Stockhausen's music if you're into pop music and you've never heard of Stockhausen, just think to yourself, 'I'm probably not going to enjoy this but nevertheless I'm just going to go for the hell of it.' And you go; you may not enjoy it but then again, it may spark something within yourself to create in your own sphere of music. So that's how I see it, I just try to open myself up to absolutely anything and everything.

Even now . . . I'm still not thinking of where I am on the ladder. Certainly I have aims and so on. For me, I'm learning music all the time, I'm coming across different musicians, playing in different places, but I'm always developing as a musician and that's my aim – to try to get to some sort of satisfaction with my playing where I can rest. I'm always nit-picking; the more you progress, the more hard you are on yourself.

I've only once moved myself by my own playing, where actually a tear dropped. I don't remember what it was or where it was; it was just an occasion. It just struck a chord and it never happened again. I doubt if it will happen. But apart from that, I finish a concert and go home and lie in bed and go through every single note. That's how critical of yourself you are. And certainly my husband, Greg, is very critical but it's nice to have someone around who can be so honest with you because it's lovely when people come up and say, 'That was brilliant', but you wonder, 'Was that out of politeness, did they really mean it?' But at the end of the day, as soon as you've walked off-stage, you know exactly how you've played; you really do. You can't hide from it; you've got to do something about it, if something hasn't gone right. It's making those little adjustments, really.

How I see things like [awards] is as a stepping-stone; it gives you the necessary encouragement to keep going, basically. And I think that's important because as a musician you have so many ups and downs and everything you do is being reviewed, criticised, written about by newspapers and so on. You go away and you know that some people will have enjoyed it and some people won't have, no matter how well you've played. That's just life. In a way, you have to be thick-skinned to cope with all of that. So things like awards are like a pat on the head really. It really allows you to work harder, to keep your aims in sight. For me, it does that; it gives me a lot of encouragement. And I think for the world of percussion, we need all the help you can get. So these awards are for the world of percussion as well; they're not just for Evelyn Glennie. For example, on the computer we log on to the World Percussion Network, and there was a review for 'Veni, Veni, Emmanuel' in the *Wall Street Journal* and some percussionist had typed up the review and put it into the network, with a little comment at the end saying, 'From all at WPN, we wish you many congratulations.' It was a nice touch; for someone to bother to type it up. It's little things like that that are important.

Rosanne Cash

R osanne Cash was born in Memphis, Tennessee, in 1955 – the same month her father, Johnny Cash, launched what would become a legendary country music career, by recording his first single at Sun Studios. Her parents' marriage ended when she was eleven. Growing up in California, her musical influences were diverse, and ranged from listening to The Beatles, Joni Mitchell and Blind Faith, to joining her father as he toured the United States.

Writing and drama were twin passions – she studied both at Vanderbilt University in Nashville and at Lee Strasberg's Theatre Institute in Los Angeles. She lived briefly in London, where she worked for CBS Records.

In 1978, she made her first record, for the Ariola label in Germany. The following year she married songwriter-producer Rodney Crowell, was signed to Columbia Records and released 'Right or Wrong' (produced by Crowell). It set the pattern for a decade of country music hits – 'Seven Year Ache' (three Number One singles on the *Billboard* magazine country music chart) in 1981, and 'Somewhere in the Stars' in 1982. A three-year hiatus followed during which two of her daughters were born. 'Rhythm and Romance' followed in 1985 and won a Grammy award. Drug abuse problems were overcome in a rehabilitation programme. 'King's Record Shop' in 1987 garnered four Number One singles, setting the record for a female country music artist; it, too, was nominated for a Grammy. On a greatest hits package in 1989, a cover of The Beatles' 'I don't want to spoil the party' reached Number One on the *Billboard* country chart. In 1988, her third daughter was born; in the same year, Billboard named her as top singles artist. 'Interiors', released in 1990, was her solo production debut and all of the material was written, or co-written, by her; it was also nominated for a Grammy. Two years later, she and Crowell divorced. In 1993 'The Wheel' was released, co-produced with John Leventhal.

Rosanne Cash has appeared in numerous musical tributes including that organised by Yoko Ono in memory of John Lennon, and the Columbia Records tribute to Bob Dylan. She was instrumental in bringing together artists like Gloria Estefan, Mary Chapin Carpenter, Emmylou Harris, Carole King and Dionne Warwick and co-produced the benefit album which featured them, 'Til Their Eyes Shine', in support of the Institute for Intercultural Understanding.

An accomplished artist, she was exhibited publicly; she is also writing a book of short stories. Rosanne Cash lives in New York City with her three daughters.

My father's music, and who he was, was so much a part of the fabric of my understanding of the world that it wasn't until I was a teenager that I had any objectivity about it. I think it's that way with any child, whatever their circumstances are, they think that's reality and then later on you find out there are other realities. But I saw what was happening, I saw that he was gone all the time and that something was wrong with him, and later knew that that was a drug problem. I'm sure somewhere I put two and two together, that there was a lot of success and him being on the road. I remember his records influencing me deeply – 'Ballads of the True West', 'Orange Blossom Special', 'Ride This Train'. As a teenager, I was really proud of him. That was when 'Folsom Prison' and 'San Quentin' came out; I remember the teacher playing them in my English class, or someone bringing them in. But he was still away all the time; he was somewhat of a distant figure and there was a lot of charge around that. [I wished] that he would be an insurance salesman, and I could go to his office and sit on his lap. That was my fantasy. I was a grown woman before I let go of that. I sat and watched him for three years from the side of the stage; what he did, how he related to an audience, what that meant. I had a real sense of him being a troubadour, he was like a folk troubadour to me. Just to see his back every night and to think, 'This could be medieval times, any time', it was timeless. Who he was and how he was; that was profoundly moving to me. I saw him as an artist and not a parent. I saw the choices that he had made as an artist because his own soul demanded it, as an artist. That's who he was; he could not be anyone else. It's who he still is. His limitations in other areas have caused him a great deal of pain but you can only be who you are. And he was that troubadour.

But, still, did I want to do that? That was a huge thing. I was at the Lee Strasberg Institute and I didn't know that I wanted to give that up. I didn't want to sing; I wanted to be a writer. I got offered this contract in Europe and I thought, 'Well, I'll interpret my own songs and I'll see how this goes and I'll try this and nobody will notice because it's in Germany!' It was purely a series of coincidences that led me to do that. I was writing songs, which was a concession; it was like, 'OK, I'm accepting this. I love music and I want to do this.' But to go and make a record . . . I couldn't get out of bed for a week. My girlfriend was taking me to doctors – 'What's wrong with her?' 'She's depressed; we don't know what's going on.' It was coming to terms with this decision; did I really want to embark on that kind of life? Because as far as I could tell, it was really destructive.

I was pretty brazen; I was living in Los Angeles, I had purple hair, I was living a rock and roll lifestyle. I made this record ['Right or Wrong']. Columbia in Nashville had signed me but I didn't feel any affiliation with Nashville. I didn't know what the community was about, I didn't know the rules. I didn't get a handbook! I went in thinking, 'Well, here I am and here it is, so that's it.' Slowly I became aware of this whole subculture and these rules and this system of hierarchies and marketing, that I had absolutely no idea about. There was nothing so overt but I began to realise they weren't embracing me; that I was a bit too much – the way I dressed, the way I looked, I had an attitude, I said 'fuck' in public. This was '79–'80, women were still playing victims in Nashville in the music scene. I didn't buy it! I rubbed a lot of people the wrong way. I assumed they would just accept me, I had no ill feelings towards anyone but I didn't realise, I was very naïve.

At the same time, I started to become very successful. 'Right or Wrong' did OK, but then 'Seven Year Ache' did really well. I withdrew! I had babies. I didn't want to tour, I didn't want to do anything. Because of my own insecurities about what I was doing, because my programming had lead me to believe that this was the road to hell and destruction, because I didn't know how to assimilate so many people having a certain image of me, because I'm by nature really private and that went against everything that I wanted for myself. And because I had a drug problem.

The main thing was, I had this burning obsession to get to the bottom of things. And when I was in the most pain, and in the most destructive state, the most unclear and the most self-deluding, I still had this burning desire to get to the truth of it, and I think that's what got me into treatment. I went to drug rehab. That's what has saved my life, if nothing else, and I give credit to God because I did say, 'Somebody that's beyond a human being has to help me'; I reached out for that and it came. It was also that desire just to know why? Why am I self-destructive? That's been the basis for my writing too; but not just my writing, that's been the basis for my life.

I think I've probably been too candid with the press; I've paid for that in some ways but at the same time, 'So what?' People are going to think what they think whether you talk or not. They [the media] burned me a couple of times. They were **doing this exposé of drug use in Nashville. It was after I was out of rehab and I didn't want to talk about it yet; I didn't want my** children to have to deal with that or my grandmother who was eighty-five years old. I said, 'I don't want to talk about it', and they put my picture on the front page of the story; it was incredibly painful. It goes to show, they're going to print what they're going to print.

I saw that I was successful but I was so defended against it changing me or hurting me that I really didn't take it in. The bad part of that was I didn't take it in to soothe myself in any way either. I never sat back and thought, 'I've really done something, now I can rest for a while.' Interestingly I don't feel like proving myself any more; at some point I think that just came with age and experience. But as far as carrying my laurels around like a sack on my back, I don't do it. Right now, I feel like I've done nothing! I think to myself, 'What have I done? I wrote a few songs. What does that mean? I'm thirty-eight years old, what am I going to do with my life?' In a way it's kind of a protective thing, it keeps you working. It keeps you honest.

I used to go to extremes about it though. I won the Burton Award for Song of the Year at BMI; a very prestigious award, for a song I'd written called 'Hold On'. I got this award and I spent the next month going over that song, saying 'This song is not, by far, the best song I ever wrote; it's weak lyrically.' Then I stopped myself; why am I expecting justice, why should the best song get this award, just accept it!

I'd gotten to the point where I didn't want to make records any more. I didn't want to make 'King's Record Shop' and Rodney talked me into it. And I got enthused because he was really inspired and had a vision for it. It was a lot of his stuff, that record. In fact, most of the records I've made with him, there was a lot of Rodney working out his stuff through me. A lot of times in the studio he would have very specific ideas and we would end up fighting about it. We fought so much in the studio! Sometimes I was content to let him work it out through me because I was inspired too. There are some things I wouldn't have chosen to do if I'd been on my own but at the same time I was learning, I was writing. I made 'King's Record Shop' and it was a huge success. And then I got pregnant right after that. I hadn't wanted to make that record; I was so burned on the record-making process and I was going through some really deep stuff internally about myself as an artist and what that meant and what I wanted to do, feeling that I'd been a dilettante up until that point, and was I going to make an internal commitment to wherever this was going to lead me, this art. I went through a major process with this. I had a dream which changed my life at that time, about meeting Art personified and him saying to me that he doesn't respect dilettantes. And it shook me to my foundations. I had the most intense identity crisis after that. So that was all going on through 'King's Record Shop'.

I still didn't want to make another record though. I let them put together this hits package and there was a couple of hit records off it, new things we had recorded. Then my marriage started falling apart. It really started falling apart when I was pregnant. You're talking about two very intense people, who haven't worked through all of their childhood shit, projecting a lot of it on to each other. I just don't know if we were different enough to make it work. We were too intense together, it always ended up being like an implosion. And it just got to be too much. I love him, I love talking to him, I love his work; it's so much easier now we're apart, to talk to each other and appreciate each other's work, to be objective about our children. When I was writing these songs, when I was going through this, then I started wanting to make a record. I saw [producer] Malcolm Burns, who listened to the demos and said, 'Why aren't you producing this yourself?' I said 'I don't know', and I just ruminated on that for a few months then I said, 'Yes, I'm going to do this.'

I was painting at the time, I was deeply into painting, I had a couple of shows; painting opened a whole new language to me, for how to make this record ['Interiors']. I could not only see it in pictures but I saw what happened in the creative process when you start dismantling yourself, or when you lose the thread and how to bring it back, through painting, and I thought I could apply this to writing and recording. So I did; I made the record, 'Interiors'. It was the first one I did on my own, the first one that I considered really 'me' all the way through. I don't think it was a departure as much as a beginning. Everything else was an accumulation of experience and knowledge and understanding about things and then I went through the turnstile; it was a really remarkable experience for me.

At the time I made it, I didn't realise it was a divorce record as [one reviewer] called it and all these people were saying all of these things that hadn't occurred to me. It was a bit shocking; maybe it did turn out to presage a divorce but at the time, it was just my music. Some of the assumptions were so off-base, too. Like the song 'Paralysed', they were saying it was about overhearing two lovers on the phone. It wasn't about that at all; it was about overhearing my parents break up when I was ten years old. While all the press were going on, and all the interviews, and they were assuming all these things, I just let them assume it, I didn't say anything. I don't know why people do that, it's some human desire, we want to know other people's specifics. I guess it makes us feel like we're OK. I've stopped worrying about it; people tend to think my work is autobiographical. It is, how could it not be? I don't get it from television! But the specifics vary and I'm not afraid to employ poetic licence.

Confronting that dark side is about getting to the bottom of things. It got very dangerous for me, during and after 'Interiors', with the things I was writing; I didn't know how to get back from that place. I had to teach myself how to get back. But it's funny, you get down so deep, to the place of your deepest woundedness, and that's when you're most closely connected with other human beings. But it's dangerous, I think that's why artists have more than their fair share of alcoholism and suicides and drug addiction because you get down in those places, you're scavenging in the deepest parts of your psyche to come up with stuff and you don't know how to get back.

It felt like some of the issues that I looked at on 'Interiors' got transformed on 'The Wheel', that some of the suffocating suffering on 'Interiors' turned into sexual rebirth, or it turned into a spiritual overview, a balancing between the spirit and the body and the soul, instead of just this single-minded focus on the emotional body. This can sound very lofty but it was a continuum to me, I felt they were bookends in a way. I thought 'The Wheel' was a kind of 'coming-out'. But it didn't do very well. I think it was chiefly, I was stigmatised by a twelve-year career, that I'd said goodbye to. I walked into the office of the president of Sony Nashville and said 'let me go' and twenty minutes later, I walked out. And I had let go of a twelve-year career. I started over with Sony in New York, thinking, 'This is going to work, they're really excited, and I can do anything I want' and then I find out, there in the real world, that radio has a certain image of me and they're not buying it.

This thing about commercial success, it's a double-edged sword and I don't know what it means any more. If I sell a million records that's a success, according to the record company, but if I sell one hundred and fifty thousand, that's a failure. But if one hundred and fifty thousand people are really moved, doesn't that mean *something*? I'm kind of in a mid-life crisis about all of this. I'm writing a book, I've already written enough material for a new album. I feel like I have a lot in my life, a lot of good things, and I have power. I don't feel like I do anything special, I've done some environmental work and some stuff for children's charities. It's out of the bounty of my life, it's not like Mother Teresa or something.

I see my teenager, like all teenagers, wanting to be special, and the centre of the universe, and her mother gets so much attention. I see that being really hard for her, or the kind of emotional terrain that I travel in order to do my work, I see that being difficult for my children. I think eventually they're happy that you have this other life but some days they just want you to be in the picture. I have been conscious about a lot of things. I certainly haven't abandoned my children to years of touring. I'm a good mother, I know I am, I'm very sensitive to my children, and what their needs are and what's going on with them and I pay attention. Because I want to be; it's an instinct to be a good mother. It just felt natural. I had my first two children, two years apart and in that two years, I stopped writing, I got really crazy because I wasn't doing anything creative and it took me a while to learn how to do both. It's still hard now! I have to steal thirty minutes if I want to write, thirty minutes here, forty there.

There were women who did it before me, like Emmylou Harris, and opened the door for me so if I wedged it a bit more for [Mary] Chapin [Carpenter], that's great. I don't think it's a mathematical formula. Maybe music journalists can say, 'At this point in the time-line, she did this and that allowed Trisha Yearwood to do this' and that would be very nice and I would love to think that but the truth is, people in Nashville aren't sitting around saying that. Why should they? Comparison does tend to kill art. Why should Jasper Johns be compared to Willem de Kooning? I never sit around thinking about that. It's only when a journalist brings it up that I think about it. It's kind of nebulous to pinpoint. Every person is unique. Hopefully there would be room for individuals and not formulas – that my brand of feminism wouldn't be the bottom line for everybody else, or yours, or Carlene's [step-sister, Carlene Carter] or Reba MacIntyre's or Chrissie Hynde's. But that there'd be room for us to disagree vehemently in our styles.

Sheila Chandra

Sheila Chandra was born in London in 1965, to Indian parents. At the age of eleven, she enrolled in the Italia Conti Academy of Theatre Arts, where for the following five years she studied music, dance and drama. She was chosen for a part in the hugely popular BBC children's series, 'Grange Hill', and remained in the series for two years.

While at the school, and becoming increasingly influenced by soul and gospel musical styles, she recorded an audition tape for Hansa Records, which was heard by songwriter and producer Steve Coe. Several months later, when Coe was searching for a vocalist for a newly formed band called Monsoon, he invited Sheila Chandra to join. A four-track EP led to a deal with the major label Phonogram. Monsoon broke new ground for British pop music in 1982 – drawing heavily on the classical structures of traditional Indian music (using drones and fixed note scales), it fused pop rhythms and a dance beat to create an idiosyncratic and unlikely Top Ten hit with its first single, 'Ever So Lonely'. Eager for a follow-up hit, Phonogram released another single, 'Shakti', but after disappointment at its failure to make it to the Top Ten (although it featured in the Top 40), creative differences between the band and Phonogram became so severe that Monsoon disbanded in late-1982. Its only album, 'Third Eye', was released posthumously the following year.

Sheila Chandra signed to Indipop to release her solo albums and began to further develop her interest in Indian music. Her first solo work, 'Out On My Own', was released in 1984; it drew on the Asian-western pop hybrid of Monsoon but showed her growing fascination with vocal experimentation, the beginnings of her 'voice as instrument' style. The follow-up, 'Quiet', released later the same year, abandoned the pop structures, expanding on the vocal textures, and was her first work to feature her own compositions.

The album, 'The Struggle', in early 1985 was upbeat and rhythm-based, structured around songs and choruses, while 'Nada Brahma', released a few months later, veered into more experimental territory, with the title track a twenty-five minute raga-like composition. At the age of twenty, after four albums in two years, Sheila Chandra began a musical and spiritual sabbatical which was to last until 1990, when she marked her return to recording with her fifth solo album, 'Roots and Wings'. The same year, a sampler album of her work to date, 'Silk', was released; she featured on an Indipop 'CompilAsian' album of Asian fusion music, and recorded with Ancient Beatbox.

In 1991, Sheila Chandra formed the production company Moonsung, and licenced the new album, 'Weaving My Ancestors' Voices', to the Real World label; the following year, she toured for the first time with the Real World sister-organisation, WOMAD. In 1993, she became Real World's largest selling artist in the United States, and featured in *Billboard* magazine's Top Ten of world music sales. The following year, Real World released her album, 'The Zen Kiss', a title she created to describe the magic of the creative experience.

Sheila Chandra lives with her husband, Steve Coe, in Somerset.

I didn't do all the socialising, the hanging-out that's associated with puberty because I just didn't have time. And it made me less self-conscious because I didn't have a peer group that I took any notice of, who were telling me I ought to behave in a certain way. I went into the adult world, where more idiosyncrasies are tolerated . . . and in a way people are interested in you because of your differences, rather than because you wear the same clothes as the fashion models. So there was a much more grown-up influence that came into my life and then, as now, it was a lot about hard work, and getting a lot of things done rather than 'hanging out'.

I was very aware that because I was the older wing of the second generation of Asians, it was the older part of the community that were watching and that I ought not really to do anything that would betray their sense of what was proper. There was so little positive coverage of Asians in the media at that time; it was mostly the problems of racism, the problems of housing, the problems of unemployment, and 'this is a problem community' in a way. Not that they might have cultural riches which were important, or that cultural diversity was important. Nearly fifteen years on, it's a very different atmosphere, [although] not different enough.

I felt that in a way, the expectations that were put on me were fairer because of the social climate than they would be if someone put those expectations on a young Asian woman entering the pop business today. Today, there is far more of an equal representation of the Asian community. Thirty-year-old media types were asking me, 'how long is a sari?' and they didn't just ask for trivial reasons, they asked because there genuinely wasn't anybody else who they felt was accessible and young, and they could talk to about simple basic things. So I did feel that I had to be a kind of cultural ambassador at that time but I threw that off later because I think that that kind of responsibility role goes too far if you carry it for too long. It was needed then, it isn't needed as much now.

I think it can be a legacy of being a second-generation Asian, it's very easy to lose your individuality, particularly when you're dealing with media people who want to be able to summarise things in a very brief way. It's very easy to get contained by that summary, and not be able to break out. When I 'retired' when I was twenty, part of the reason was because I'd done all this work in the adult world – I did 'Grange Hill', I did the Monsoon album and I did the four solo albums all before I was twenty – apart from a [physical] break, I also needed a break from all of the reflections that were coming back at me. I needed to really assess myself as an individual and to check that those expectations weren't actually limiting the path that my life would take, to check that all the voices in my head were *my* voices rather than the voices of conditioning that came from exterior expectations.

[My parents] understood being a pop star and wanting to release singles and when Monsoon was successful and it was a more accessible type of music, they were happy with that. But when Monsoon disbanded and I decided I wanted to go and make albums, to sign to an independent [record company] and not release singles or be on TV every other minute, they didn't really understand that. I think it takes a lot of bravery from parents to be able to both understand and accept your child as an artist if your family is not one that's artistic, and mine wasn't. Because that person is going to continually question everything and if you're a family whose identity is bound up in certain patterns of thought, patterns of loyalty, then that can become very threatening to the family. So when they worked out what it meant in terms of my own mental freedom, they were not as comfortable with that, and it led to me breaking off communication with them eventually.

Being an artist sometimes demands bravery and courage of you. It isn't obvious because you're not scaling mountains or bungee-jumping, which literally physically gets your heart racing, but in terms of deciding, almost in a very ruthless fashion, that your own individuality is the most important thing, that your own artistic integrity is the most important thing, and arranging your life so that none of those things are compromised or limited in any way, that takes bravery and it takes some harsh decisions.

Monsoon set the scene for me, in a lot of ways, because they had this premise of combining Indian classical music with British pop music that I really wanted to explore. [I was] like a kid in a toy shop, really, having total freedom. Steve Coe, who had formed the Indipop label, initially to help Monsoon get off the ground, to get Phonogram's attention, kept the label going for me. At that point, he had fourteen years' music business experience, and I was new to it. I was seventeen or eighteen, and I didn't want to be bothered with the business side of it. I wanted to get on with doing my own musical apprenticeship, because although I had five years of theatre arts training, I'd obviously had nothing to prepare me for this particular field of music, and there is no one you can go to, to learn from, you really have to make your own experiments, and evolve your own rules and principles. So he took care of the business platform so there was a clear space where I could make albums, they would be put out, they would be mildly promoted, there would be no singles, and not a lot of time spent on promotion, but somewhere where there were absolutely no marketing or commercial pressures on me to produce anything commercial, but just to produce what was going on within me.

[One reviewer] recently said, 'Sheila put out her first four solo albums on her husband, Steve Coe's, Indipop label', which is like saying, 'Sheila, blonde, twenty-four, unmarried. Offers please!' He wasn't my husband when he put out the albums! It was just his [the reviewer's] way of belittling it. Let's forget that she initially signed to Phonogram, let's infer that she couldn't get a deal anywhere else!

I started to write my second solo album, 'Quiet', in 1984. It's when my voice became more of a leading force really, because I write on my voice and it was natural that I wanted to explore what my voice could do as an instrument. So 'Quiet' was many, many layers of vocal riffs overlaid. That was really the beginning of the experiments which led me to 'Weaving My Ancestors' Voices' and 'The Zen Kiss'.

It was part of finding my identity as a musician to be able to go in several different directions. The albums jumped around in terms of the themes that they explored and if you play them chronologically, they do sound very different to each other. I think also, having grown up when I did, I didn't know anything other than the [pop] charts. I didn't know about independents, I didn't know about serious rock musicians, I didn't know about concept albums. I associated a few women with experimentation but not very many, and I didn't really associate albums with women.

It felt to me that it was very important to give myself a chance to do some very serious experimentation and to get away from the 'pretty' side of things, both vocally and in terms of image, and in terms of doing things that are accessible – to overplay that, because I think that people do put that on you when you're a woman. They put it more on Kylie Minogue than they would on Jason Donovan, although to me they're both exactly the same. We talk about women being too pretty but we don't so often talk about how pretty and well-crafted men's images are. There should be more of an equality of perception about that kind of thing.

Record companies can't be entirely blamed because they are up against that media wall. I think record companies have their hands forced by the [BBC] Radio One playlist policy or 'we'll only play singles because England is a singles-led market' and so on. It's been important for me to go abroad to places where playlists and programming policies aren't quite as difficult. For instance, in America, where college and public radio stations have always picked up on my work and played it a lot and have got my name known to a far wider variety of people, just because they're willing to say, 'We like having an eclectic programming policy because we think it makes us interesting.'

I'd been very quiet as a child; music and voice were really my primary means of expression. If I wanted to express myself, I'd do it through a song rather than be particularly articulate. So it was important for me to crystallise things in words; I think it made me more articulate afterwards to go through that kind of process and it was very good for ironing out things. It felt like going through your sock drawer and finding an odd sock and saying, 'That doesn't belong there, where does that come from!' That kind of mental house-cleaning was overdue, because I'd spent so long working. In a way, it made me braver about music because I started to think more in terms of emotions, feelings, and about what I wanted to express, and how creative and courageous I wanted to be.

I'd gone through the 'toy shop' stage by then, I'd gone through a lot of recording techniques and instruments and structures that I wanted to explore in purely mechanical terms. So 'Roots and Wings', 'Weaving My Ancestors' Voices' and 'The Zen Kiss', which were the three albums that followed that break, show a more holistic side, because I'd really had a chance to explore the mechanical bits.

What I was doing on 'Quiet', 'Struggle' and 'Nada Brahma' was really finding different settings for my voice and experimenting almost in the way that you would with a mosaic, learning to put things where I wanted them. I spent a lot of time working on my voice and working on my vocal techniques because I hadn't really had time to do that. When I came out with 'Roots and Wings' there were tracks like 'One' which had twenty-three tracks of weaved cyclic vocals, and I thought 'This is the end, I'll never ever be able to play live!' I wasn't a great fan of live performances up until that point but I started to slowly become fascinated with that feeling that people have when they're recounting their favourite live concert story, that incredible twinkle they've got in their eyes, when they're relating how that moved them. And you think, 'Why? OK, they can see the person playing but that's the only difference between concerts and a studio. What is the magic?' The idea that there might be something intangible, there might be something magical about a person's physical presence when they're playing music, became more and more a lure to me. What I sensed was that the audience wanted to feel the total involvement, feel being lost in the music, but in a way through the performer, to have their own sense of attention deepened by the performer's insight. So when I decided to play live I wanted to do it completely alone because I really wanted to heighten that situation between myself and the audience.

I wrote a new batch of material which turned out to be 'Weaving My Ancestors' Voices', which was all solo voice with the occasional drone so that I could go out on-stage completely alone and learn about that process, and it was really great. The first performance was very scary. But in a way, it's very powerful, no one can take anything away from you. It's the sort of thing that people know you could do in a front room, almost as well as on-stage, and you don't need lots and lots of trappings. It's nice if you have a good acoustic space, it enhances if I'm singing Gregorian chanting going into Vedic chanting, to be able to change the acoustic environment by delays and reverbs. The voice and the environment become one instrument. I don't have to turn around to musicians and say, 'I'm going to do this number now, I'm going to change the running order.' I can do exactly what I want, I can edit or improvise. Once you can do that, you can face most situations.

I don't like this strong performer/audience barrier that there is. I don't like that [attitude of], 'she's up there, and we're down here and we can't do what she does, and we're supposed to be quiet'. The silence is nice when you're doing something that really needs silence as a backdrop as a lot of my stuff does, but I like the idea that people might go away feeling empowered to do what I do. And I give away all my vocal secrets in workshops or lectures, as soon as I know them so that I don't hold anything back, because I really want people to understand the complexities in the music, but also go and try it themselves and go and experience what I've been experiencing.

Because I'd found a way of going between different vocal traditions without having to pause or take a breath or go into a different song, I wanted to emphasise how this vocal heritage, this musical heritage, is really for everyone, and there really is no geographical or cultural barrier that should stand in the way. I'm respectful about the music that I draw from and I don't think it would be valid for me to say to someone, for instance, who had no cultural Asian connection, 'you can't do that'. In a shrinking world, I just don't think that that is right anymore. I don't think it's weird or freakish to become totally absorbed in another culture's music or music that has very strong influences from another culture.

The songs are usually explorations of things that are going on in my head. Occasionally, those things are to do with my own experience, most of the time they're to do with music that I'm hearing in my head, that I can't go out and buy. My musical space, the space I go into when I'm writing and when I'm performing, is about leaving behind, but not escaping, the fact that I'm female, the fact that I'm Asian, the fact that I look the way I do, all those sorts of things which one might think made for a limitation in life or my thinking. I go to another place where I don't consider those things and it gives me a kind of lateral shift so that I can come up with ideas that I couldn't if I was stuck down on the ground within all of those social constraints. Everyone needs to be that creative, to leap out of the way they look, or the way they come across and have the chance to, in a way, reinvent themselves, to be what they want to be, to let their true spirit and their true potential shine out of that. Because my music is about that, it's very irritating when interviewers or reviewers insist on putting a lot of personal details in, because I think 'What has *that* got to do with it, with the world I go into!'

A lot of the elements come to me by chance. Someone played me a CD of the works of Abbess Hildegard and someone sang me 'Donalogue', and said, 'You've got the kind of voice that would sing this song really well.' 'The Zen Kiss' took two years to write and I think you need a greater density of ideas for a solo voice album because you can't rely on the connotations that say, strings have . . . you've got to make sure that everything is very crafted. With 'La Sagesse', I actually had to create a new song structure in order to fit Arabic vocal and gospel vocal together, so it's challenging things on a structural level and that takes a lot of work for it to seem effortless to the listener, and for it to be familiar and draw on enough inherently known structure, culturally known structure – that verse, chorus, verse, chorus thing – without actually conforming to that so that I could get the Arabic vocals in as well.

The experience that 'The Zen Kiss' is trying to describe is a feeling when I'm on-stage or when I'm rehearsing or sometimes when I'm writing, where it feels like I'm being taken over and as though a kind of higher intelligence is using my voice to sing a song in a way that I could not have contrived with my conscious intelligence. Every note is perfect and I think . . . 'this is what I've been working towards'. I don't know if I'll be able to repeat it, it just feels so brilliant. My talent is that I have the ability to feel that experience more within singing than within anything else, and maybe that's what the definition of talent is – that one is able to connect, in a way, to a higher force and let the thing be done through you.

I know everybody has the capacity to feel it in their own areas of talent. And I know that I've felt it some days when everything seems to have gone right and I've been really involved, even if it's mundane, I've felt great satisfaction. And the word 'Zen' seemed to be the closest thing that describes that experience. In a way, you become the thing: If I fight for my identity, 'I must get this vocal right!' The more I think like that, the more disjointed the vocal grows. When I stop thinking in words and I almost *become* the song because I'm listening to it so intently, that's when it seems to happen.

With women, there is a great dilemma because a lot of that unaccompanied singing has been kept going by women, because the voice is the instrument, and I happen to think, as in the Indian musical tradition, that the treble and the harmonics of a woman's voice make it an inherently superior singing instrument. I think that's why women's voices are more popular. It's the instrument we've always got, we've had access to, it's the instrument we're biologically tied to and it's therefore a very emotional instrument that can be, if you know how to use it well, a true mirror to what we're feeling. So, I think of the voice as a woman's instrument, in the best way, in the way that women excel at it.

[There are] places where women are excluded, for instance, where the muezzin call from the tower, where it's not actually law that women can't learn, but they'd have to be in contact with men within a mosque so it's impractical. But I think women's voices sound superior doing that kind of thing.

Women in so-called 'world' music, if they are actually living in a country where the culture is still traditional, and if it's a sexist culture as well, have a double barrier to face . . . Even though there isn't, in this society, a physical pressure on you, that if you think differently you'll go to jail, or get sent to Siberia, I think there still is a cultural and a social pressure to conform and particularly for women. This [attitude of] 'sound pretty, be accessible and don't be dangerous'; or, 'we won't call you dangerous, we'll call you mad, and that way we can shut you off or ignore you, and say that your work isn't worth anything, and we won't allow you to challenge us then. You're a woman, you're not supposed to be like that!'

There are all these old folk tunes, with 'I'll do your milking and I'll nurse your baby' and all that . . . 'Donalogue' was like that so I decided to change the lyrics so I could actually sing it without having to put any rubbish through my brain. I won't sing Tamla Motown songs which are all about the dependence of 'I'm waiting by the phone . . . my life is incomplete until you're here!'

I just think the voice ought to be, at some time, heard in its full flower, where there's nothing else in the sound spectrum, and where human emotion and ingenuity, and the human sampler, in my case, is the ultimate point. The 'Speaking in Tongues' pieces are borne out of the kind of ineptitude that I've heard with sampling in the early days, and you still hear sometimes. In a way, it made clipped beats and slight dissonance more OK to mainstream ears. Dissonance exists pretty much in the Indian tradition and is used to convey certain emotions but you didn't really hear dissonance in the pop tradition, but because people weren't aware of the key they were sampling from and the key they were moving to, they allowed that through, and it was really delightful and refreshing. I wanted to really explore that with things like 'Speaking in Tongues' where you're constantly chopping things up, you're deliberately ignoring bar-lines, deliberately talking about chaos and bringing something up out of the unborn and how mad it feels to be an artist sometimes, and how you worry, 'Am I the only person that feels this?'

———————————————— ■ ————————————————

I find kindred spirits all over the place and I find them sometimes where I least expect them. In the music business as well, I find odd souls, men and women, who stand up for what they believe in and for what they like, and for what's not necessarily trendy, what is deep and what has real musical value. They have a tough time of it, but it's very inspiring. In a way, it's an isolated position to be in as an artist, but one can, without necessarily having a support group, be inspired by what someone does from afar. I know that at times when I've been low, to see someone else's brave act, to see someone else make a brave record, has given me strength. Your statement does matter even if you think it's not touching anybody; it does, on a level that you can never know. As well as making yourself stronger, for having integrity with what is really the truth about yourself.

I can't stand achievement culture and that's why there are certain men and women in the music business who inspire me because they're not achievement-oriented, they're not about punishing themselves physically and mentally time after time in order to achieve consistency with their colleagues, or ignoring the fact that they have a family, or that they have a soul. That's not to say that one has to be irresponsible or unreliable, but I think this constant 'do more hours, build up more pressure, you are what you achieve, look at your status or money', all of those carrot/stick things . . . It takes bravery and I don't opt out of this out of any sense of heroism, I do it because I really can't be any other way, and it can feel very cold and lonely out on the edge where there are no promotions and no points and no status, other than your own sense of knowing that you've grown as a person.

[I] manage myself, own my own recordings and licence them to Real World on a one-off basis, which means that I'm not beholden to them for any other [album]. Maybe it's not a plateau that gives me as much access to as much of a publicity budget, or as much of a high profile as other mainstream performers, but it is an area that I can truly call my own. It is important to get very practical about the business side of things so you are absolutely on firm ground, and able to control what you do, otherwise you find yourself in the situation where you're signed to the record company for the next record, they're insisting they release a single, they're insisting that you re-mix the track, or they'll throw the whole album out. You're completely on shaky ground. Doing what I'm doing isn't possible without getting practical about it.

Carla Bley

C arla Bley was born in Oakland, California, in 1938. Her parents were both musicians; her father, the organist and choir-master at their local church, also taught piano. Her mother died when Carla was eight. She began composing as a young child, influenced by hymns and classical music, writing part of an opera ('Over the Hill') at the age of nine. At the age of twelve, her life was dominated by roller-skating, and she competed in Californian state championships. She left school at fifteen to work in a music shop and joined forces with a folk-singer, writing songs and performing in night-clubs. At seventeen, she left California, travelling with a friend to New York City. There, penniless and homeless, she lived briefly in Grand Central railway station before getting a job selling cigarettes at one of the city's most famous jazz clubs – Birdland, named after jazz legend, Charlie Parker. Here, she watched her heroes – Miles Davis, Charles Mingus, Count Basie, Thelonius Monk and Anita O'Day.

At Birdland, she met Canadian musician Paul Bley, who she married. She continued writing and was playing New York's jazz clubs in a band with saxophonist Pharaoh Saunders, and drummer Charles Moffett. Bley himself recorded her works as did numerous others, including Art Farmer, George Russell, Jimmy Guiffre and Charlie Haden.

By the early '60s, frustrated with the commercial aspects of the music industry, she joined the Jazz Composers Guild. The Guild was short-lived but one of its principles – to support and promote composers writing for large ensembles – was carried on when she created the Jazz Composers Orchestra with Mike Mantler, her second husband. The JCO was a loose grouping of mainly New York-based musicians dedicated to putting free jazz in an orchestral context. Shortly after the JCO was formed, she helped to organise the Jazz Composers Orchestra Association, a non-profit group set up to support the JCO and to commission and record new works. In 1965 Bley and Mantler presented their Jazz Composers Workshop in New York.

After failing to interest any major record companies in their innovative and experimental work, Bley played on the first JCO release, Mike Mantler's 'The Jazz Composers Orchestra' in 1968; other featured players included Don Cherry, Gato Barbieri, Pharaoh Saunders and Cecil Taylor. The album sold well in Europe and Japan but sales in the United States were hampered by lack of interest from distributors. The following year Carla Bley arranged the music for Charlie Haden's 'Liberation Music Orchestra', a fifty-minute piece based on music from the Spanish Civil War.

In 1967 she had composed 'A Genuine Tong Funeral' for Gary Burton, and begun work on a magnum opus, 'Escalator over the Hill', which was written with the poet Paul Haines and appeared as a triple album in 1972. It is credited as the largest complete work to have emerged within jazz. Among the featured singers and players were Jack Bruce, Linda Ronstadt, John McLaughlin, Don Cherry, Roswell Rudd and Charlie Haden. With a jazz base, the work incorporated elements of rock, Indian and Eastern traditional music.

Deciding to circumvent the strictures of mainstream distributors, Bley and Mantler set up the New Music Distribution Service, a non-profit service that encouraged artists who were playing or writing experimental new music, giving them a distribution network without the commercial pressures to compromise their work. By the end of the '70s, the NMDS catalogue boasted more than two hundred titles, from fifty record companies. Their artists included Laurie Anderson, Chick Corea, Philip Glass and Gil Scott-Heron.

In 1975, after performing in Europe as part of ex-Cream

bass-player Jack Bruce's band, Bley became increasingly involved in writing for her own Big Band, and recording on the Watt label which she and Mantler had started two years earlier. Her Big Band has grown from a fifteen-piece ensemble to the Very Big Band of nineteen players, including her daughter, Karen.

Bley's recording career covers more than thirty albums as a band leader, composer and player. Among her dozens of commissions has been a mini-opera based on Malcolm Lowry's novel, *Under the Volcano*, and the work 'Birds of Paradise', which was commissioned by the city of Glasgow and filmed for a BBC documentary.

Carla Bley lives near Woodstock, New York.

———————————————————— ■ ————————————————————

I'm not sure if I showed musical talent as a child; my father was a piano teacher, so he just automatically taught me to play, as though he was teaching me to talk or walk. I may not have had any talent whatsoever, though I guess I still wouldn't be around if I hadn't! I had a really interesting and good childhood. When my mother died, it wasn't a big deal, she'd been sick all of her life, and if anything, it was a release. So I don't feel I had anything but a totally charmed childhood.

When you're that young you don't go into anything, and it was too late, by the time I'd reached an age where I could decide what to do; I was a dyed-in-the-wool musician, so I have no idea what would have happened otherwise. But I enjoyed music. I'll tell you one thing, I wasn't as good as I thought I was! I thought I was the only wonderful child musician in the world and when my father entered me in some kind of a competition I was one of the very worst in the city of Oakland! That was a bit of a shock! I was nine or ten. Then, I realised that I didn't have any discipline, and I didn't want any, so I didn't really start being disciplined until much later – like five years ago, maybe! I just did whatever I wanted to do, for most of my life.

From a very early age, my father let me do whatever I

wanted to do. When I had a birthday party, I could have hay in the house, and have a hay party! And if I wanted to ride my bicycle at three in the morning, on the streets of Oakland, I could do that. I was [allowed] to grow totally wild and it was wonderful, it was really fun.

Music only left [my life] for the years between fourteen and sixteen, when I was a roller-skater. I became interested in roller-skating, and I was in a California state competition and was placed seventh in the free-style. Naturally, it was *free*-style, I couldn't do anything disciplined! I wasn't very good but it consumed me for two years, I just wanted to roller-skate. It wasn't hard, it was just fun, twirling around, jumping around, it was like my sport. Then I quit doing that and music reared back up into first place and it's sort of stayed there.

When I was skating, I had a job playing piano for a dance studio, I was fourteen. I was skating, I was still going to school, and after school, I was going to Berkeley from Oakland on the bus and playing piano at a dance studio. Then, when I quit school at fifteen, I took a job in a music store, I thought that would be a musical job but of course it wasn't, it was selling sheet music and metronomes. I would just quit jobs, I never felt it was necessary to stick to anything. As soon as I didn't like it any more, I would quit. Then, I started getting jobs in night-clubs as a musician. There were a couple of night-clubs in San Francisco – the Hungry Eye and the Purple Onion – they were pretty famous at that time, and I got jobs there as an accompanist for a guy who sang and wrote folk-songs. I'd help him write, he'd sing the melodies to me and I'd write them down with the changes and make it into a song. And I started to get paid for that, so that became a way to make a living at that point. And I travelled a little around the country, with this guy playing at different night-clubs.

I didn't actually quit school until fifteen but I quit going to school a long time before then, just staying on the bus instead of getting off at the correct bus-stop. I didn't like school at all, it wasn't interesting for me. Once again, it was just a lack of having to buckle down and do things I didn't like. Now, I can do that, I can do things I don't like but it took a long time because as a child, I wasn't taught to do anything I didn't like to do. So, it was a mistake probably. Luckily I've lived long enough to make some corrections and now I'm OK! But I didn't have many skills, and I didn't have any tolerance for pain, unhappiness, boredom or things that you're taught to get through when you're a child.

It wasn't just me because ten years later, in the '60s, to drop-out became the thing to do. When I quit high school I was the only person to quit, that I knew. No one said anything, I had no friends to speak of, and no one would have dared say anything to me, I wouldn't have listened. My father didn't say anything, he let me do whatever I wanted to do. I didn't have peers, I didn't really have parents, I didn't take life seriously. I wish I had taken it more seriously, I'd like to try it again to see what would happen if I'd stayed in school. It might not turn out as good as this, it's turned out pretty good for me but it might have turned out better. Maybe I might have been a rocket scientist!

I wasn't a disciplined musician at all, maybe that's why I was such a good composer. Because I had no reins on my imagination whatsoever and I just pursued whatever note was in my head, followed by whatever note came next, followed by whatever instrumentation I was interested in, just a total lack of any strictures, any parameters, the lack of everything except 'do what you feel like doing'. And I'm just lucky that that worked for me – and it didn't for a long time. This was before jazz. This was after I quit school. A couple of years later, I felt I'd made a big mistake, that I should have stayed in. I could've got a job, I wouldn't have had to be a waitress. But it was too late then . . . and I've never even got a high school equivalency, I've remained uneducated.

At seventeen, I went to New York and that was a real adventure. I met the son of the concert-master of the Boston Symphony Orchestra, in Monterey, California. We borrowed a gasoline credit card from a room-mate of his, took one loaf of bread and one brick of cheese from the ice-box and went to New

York in this car. We ate virtually nothing but bread and cheese, and got the gas with the credit card. So that's how I got to New York for the first time. Then, of course we had nowhere to live. We didn't have a romantic relationship, it was just a friendly relationship and we split ways when we got to New York. I went to live in Grand Central Station as a homeless person – forty years before homeless people were the rage. But then, there were other homeless people, they were all very, very insane.

I had no money at all and no friends at all but one thing would lead to another. It wasn't strength, it was just ignorance of what could happen to me. And just that old free spirit. I'd think, 'I'll do this now'. Then I got a job at Birdland, as a cigarette-girl and I got to hear all the music. I got all my musical education for free and I got paid for it.

I decided to be a jazz musician long before I worked at Birdland, that's why I got a job there, because I wanted to hear these guys [Miles Davis, Thelonius Monk] play. I decided I wanted to be a jazz musician in California long before I took that loaf of bread and brick of cheese and got in that car. I had heard just a little bit. I had heard Lionel Hampton at the Oakland Auditorium and I thought, 'Wow, that is *so* great!' And [I'd seen] Gerry Mulligan and Chet Baker in San Francisco at the Black Hawk, and I thought, 'That is *so* cool!' Of course, I didn't realise that I wasn't really that 'qualified' [to play jazz]. But once again, I couldn't be stopped – nothing sunk in, no warning, no information, even if it was given, I don't even remember anyone giving me warnings or talking to me at all, I was just in a world of my own. And absorbing all this music.

I had no idea that I didn't 'qualify'. Anita O'Day was singing at Birdland at that time, and what a hero she was to me. And she swore, she used four-letter words, and I'd never even heard any of them and I was so fascinated with the words she was using and the tough way she talked to other musicians. I admired her – why couldn't I be like Anita O'Day? Of course I wasn't very tough and I just had one dress – it was a little green and white striped cotton pinafore that I had made myself. This is what I wore in the night-clubs, this one dress which had just shredded by that point. So I really didn't resemble a woman of that world at all. But you know something? Nobody ever said, 'What are you doing here?' There is something about the jazz world – knock on wood! – that is incredibly fair. It's easy to tell if you can play, and if you can write, there's the evidence. And if you're two feet tall with blue skin, it's not as important in the jazz world as it is in the pop world! I had no problem, and I've never had a problem. I never had any prejudice.

I think maybe it was just that I was not a typical woman, or maybe not a typical anything. A lot of women came up to me later and said, 'How can I become a jazz musician?' And I said, 'You're too short, for one thing, and your feet are too small!' I'd just say stupid things like that – you're not a strong person if you have to ask somebody how to belong somewhere. I never asked anybody how to belong or if I could belong. You can't, just because you're a minority, all of a sudden be allowed in. You have to be really good, and different. I was just very sure of what I was doing and I never had to change, I never had to talk tough.

Finally, I met a musician [Paul Bley] who liked me enough to take me out of Birdland. He took me to his hotel-room, to begin with! He rescued me from a job that was going nowhere because I only made enough money to pay the Times Square hotel every week. There was no way I could ever get out of there, I would have been doing it today, if somebody hadn't taken me out of there. So he put me to work in night-clubs playing the piano; I didn't play very well but I managed to get paid. People would ask me to play a popular song and I knew about twenty-five songs, so that got me through a lot of situations and made a lot more money.

I really started writing seriously with Paul Bley because he wanted songs, and he knew I was writing but I wasn't ever doing anything with them. So he would say, 'I need five songs for tomorrow' and I would write them overnight. When he recorded, he would record my songs so I started writing for him.

Through his connections, probably, I got pieces recorded by other musicians. The first stuff was recorded by [him], then Jimmy Guiffre, whose band Paul was in, and by George Russell, and Paul Bley also knew him. Then after that, it was Steve Swallow who showed Art Farmer those tunes, and told Gary Burton about me. So, to a large extent, it was the players that I knew who were telling the band-leaders. I don't think that could have happened today. That was a rare period in time, where bands had composers write music for them. Now, I think almost all band-leaders just write their own, that's where the copyright royalties are, and in the jazz world it's very hard to make it just as a player. If you're not a composer, if you don't get the copyright royalties and the performance royalties for written music, you can't really make a decent living. So everyone has had to start writing their own tunes.

I was a writer to begin with, and I had the freedom not to play which is backwards to the way most people work – the players who had the freedom not to write, then they had to start writing. But in a way, it caught up with me because I had to start playing. When the style changed no longer did people come by my house and say, 'Have you got a waltz, what's the latest blues you wrote?' They'd take what they wanted and record it and I'd get paid for it but when that stopped happening, in the '70s, I knew I was going to have to have my own band in order to play the songs I was writing, or they would never get played. So, in '77, I started having my own band, playing these songs and recording them, and that's how I made it in the jazz world. I had to do both things – I had to play as well as write.

When I lead a band, I'm no Buddy Rich: I say, 'Oh, could you please try that a little better . . . I'm sure it wasn't wrong, I'm sure you know it better than I do but if you just try it one other way, I'd be so grateful thank you, thank you!' So I have this weird style of getting the guys to do what I want them to do, without toughening up. I've never toughened up. It's no lie, sometimes I really am embarrassed about asking these great musicians that I play with, to do something differently. It's not as though I'm putting on an act, I'm being natural, I'm being myself. And I haven't had to change.

The last five years the size [of the band] has been nineteen people. The more the better! The more appeal, the more fun it is, and the more you feel like you're in your own home. [The music] is pretty carefully written out. Only four people are allowed to improvise – I give little tiny spots to all the guys in the band – but basically, I have my four soloists who I trust and the rest of the guys are reading music and doing exactly what they're supposed to do. This is something I've worked out in the last five years and it works for me very well. I really like my four soloists a lot and they really get a lot of freedom in how to express the phrases, of course total freedom during their solo. The only rules I apply are after the fact, during the mix, or choosing the tapes to be used.

About five years ago, I started trying to become a piano player and now, I practise for a half-hour in the morning, and I'm a piano player, I'm sort of enjoying it. I said [to myself] 'OK, it's time for some discipline, for the first time. I hope you have it in you!' And I do, I can practise. It's fun and it's easier than writing music, you just run your hands up and down with the metronome going or read written exercises, it's a lot easier.

I had been writing music since I was very, very young. I had composed the beginning of an opera when I was nine, called 'Over the Hill'. It was just the beginning, only a couple of songs, it wasn't a real opera. [The opera] 'Escalator over the Hill' was a total coincidence; it was named by Paul Haines, the lyricist. Ten years later, I thought, "Over the Hill", that's so weird!' but it's a coincidence.

I wrote ['Escalator'] before I knew much about music, that was written in such ignorance . . . there was no idea behind it, I don't know why, I just did it. Paul Haines, who was a friend of mine, a poet whose work I liked very much, had moved to India and had sent me a poem that was fantastic. At that moment, I was writing a piece and miraculously, the words of his poem fitted right into the piece that I was working, without any changes. It was called 'Detective Writer Daughter' and I thought the title was beautiful anyway. I played the words to the poem on the piano, and I thought, 'this goes together!' and I had never written words to anything before, not since I was five. I wrote back to him and said, 'Let's write an opera'. Just like that! He sent me more poems and I made an opera out of them; he sent about twenty-two pieces of paper, and I wrote music to them. I didn't know it would be that big, I thought it would be just one record. I tried to get someone to buy it but no one would so while I waited it became two [records] and by the time I got the money together to do it myself, it was really long. But that was not the intention, it just got longer while I waited.

I was writing 'A Genuine Tong Funeral' about three years before it was recorded [in 1967]. I started writing that in Europe. Then I became pregnant, and I still don't think my life changed at all when I had a kid. I just kept touring anyway, and brought her [Karen Mantler] with me. I didn't have a band of my own yet but I was playing with other people, and she just came with us. From the age of four months, she was on the road with me and nothing changed whatsoever. We would either hire a baby-sitter to come with us on the tour to watch her while I was on-stage, or check her in the cloakroom – one or other of those irreverent things! We were sort of irreverent about children. When she was old enough to go to boarding-school, at the age of five, we put her in a boarding-school in upstate New York, just an hour away from us; a lot of other musicians' children were there. It was a great, crazy Summerhill-type school. She only came home every other week, so then we could tour. That went on until she was ten. Then, she would tour with me, just playing glockenspiel or something like that.

I didn't encourage her to play but she started on her own pretty much, so I put her in the band but it wasn't the other way around. I didn't even teach her to play the piano or anything, I didn't give her lessons; that she became a musician was really nothing to do with me. I wanted her to become a dentist or something! Now she's a waitress – that's what happens to musicians who don't make a living. A dentist would have been better! I never told her what to do, she was raised just as loosely as I was.

Jazz Composers Orchestra was a political idea, really, that anyone who wanted to write for an orchestra of jazz musicians should be allowed to. And we raised money from rich people – we said this is a great idea, isn't it? And they said 'yes!' and gave us money. So Mike [Mantler] did the first recording for Jazz Composers Orchestra and I did the second one and we said, 'OK, somebody better do the third one.' And we thought Don Cherry might like to do it. We said, 'We'll give you this money if you write an album for Jazz Composers Orchestra.' Then we thought who do we get next? It turned out there was only about five people who wanted to do this so we stopped doing it. We knew we couldn't do it again because that wasn't the concept. Although I claim that I don't have ideas, OK that was an idea, a political idea not a musical idea.

Then we had to start Watt [record company] because it wouldn't have been fair to do another recording on the JCO label, because that was supposed to be for everybody – even though there was nobody more to do. So we started our own label, and a lot of other people started their own labels too. Then we started the New Music Distribution Service and, for many years, coped with the amount of recordings being made by musicians independently and tried to distribute them. We ended in ruin [in 1991] . . . by not being smart, by doing things without thinking them through, just lack of control. We did do a lot of good, we started a lot of people off like Chick Corea, Laurie Anderson, Philip Glass, John Zorn, Gil Scott-Heron. For ten years we distributed the records that nobody else wanted – 'If nobody wants it, bring it to us, we want it!' As we slowly went broke: 'We don't care if it sells or not, we'll take it anyway!' It was madness.

We wanted people to graduate from us and the best thing

that could happen was when they left us – that was better than staying because it meant they were successful. Everything was backwards! Because it costs more to distribute a bestselling record. The first good-selling record was Chick Corea's 'Return to Forever' and we couldn't handle it, we had just three people in the office. 'Winter in America' by Gil Scott-Heron was the second one, once again there was an undercurrent and people had heard it on the radio, everyone wanted it all of a sudden. We could not keep up and neither could Gil Scott-Heron. He said, 'I don't have the bread to get them pressed!'

I'm a record company as well as an artist so I have to be two different people. As a record company, I want to sell as many records as I can. As an artist, I don't really care at all but since I have to be both people, you could say half of me really wants to sell more because I'm still at the stage, just like with distributing records, where it costs more for me to make a record than it's worth. So I have to subsidise my recordings with performances.

It's news to me that I have the respect of critics; I don't think so: I'm not aware of that, I think they give me a hard time. I'm always a little nervous about the reviews not being good. I'm not aware of being loved by them . . . but I think it does happen more in Europe than the States. I wasn't in the [American] Encyclopaedia of Jazz until recently. Ten years ago, I certainly wasn't. [The editor] didn't like me at all! He once saw my band when we were singing, it was during that stage where we were singing awful songs like 'Hot River', we never recorded them but we were having a good time, singing stupid songs. He heard [us] and thought it was disgusting and thought it wasn't jazz, so wouldn't put me in the encyclopaedia! Isn't that awful? He had no sense of humour! But I think in Europe, I am regarded as a United States' national treasure but not here in the United States!

No jazz musician is very big here [in the US]. In general, [people] don't require as sophisticated a kind of music as the

Europeans or Japanese. Although we have a good time playing special spots in the United States like colleges, and Nashville is fantastic . . . we play ten or fifteen times in the States all year long, that's all, but they're always really good gigs. That's the way we like it, we don't like to travel in the States anyway, the food's no good, the hotels aren't great, it's just not as sensual as travelling in all of the different European countries. There's just little things about each country that are so exciting and so different.

I like to think that I'm the one reaching out to the audience and they don't have to do any reaching. But then I wouldn't be a good judge of that because to me, my music is perfectly ordinary. It depends on the state of your ears if this music is what you get enjoyment from, you come and hear it, it doesn't mean that you have to work harder when you listen to this music, it just means that you're the type of person who enjoys it more. Enjoyment is the primary thing, you must enjoy it. I hope no one's ever there because they think they should enjoy it – that's like classical music, not my concerts!

———————————————————■———————————————————

When I write for classical musicians I write just the same stuff I write for jazz musicians so you could say it's eclectic in terms of the kind of people who play it, but the music is just my music, I don't think it changes too much. You start with an idea, a bar or a couple of bars. 'Birds of Paradise', which was commissioned by the city of Glasgow, was different because that was originally for a string quartet. Steve [Swallow] and I had decided we wanted to add a string quartet to our duets. I spent a long time trying to write for a string quartet, and failing. So I took a lot of the melodies and made it into a big band violin piece. That doesn't always work, but it worked then.

Once I had 'Birds of Paradise', I had to write enough big band music for another recording, and I had to write another forty minutes of music – fifty-five minutes of music took two years of writing, two years of hard work. I'm very, very slow now. It's because I quit smoking! So I can't sit at the piano for as long as I used to be able to and I can't concentrate as well. It's been more than three years now, so I don't worry about it, I'm over it! But it slowed my pace down from ten hours a day to two hours a day and now I'm trying to work back up to it. But it's good, that's why I'm also having more fun playing because when you're playing, you don't need to smoke. But when you're writing music, it's a wonderful thing to have a cigarette between thoughts. But when I quit smoking, it slowed me way down.

It's just terror until you get it [done] and I'm so happy when I *finish* anything. I'm happy when I finish the set at a concert, I'm happy when I finish a piece of music, I'm happy when I finish a recording. I'm not happy during the writing, playing, or recording of it at all, I just think, 'Oh, God, it's not going to work out', or 'it's awful!' I don't enjoy the process at all. I don't think I'm as good as I should be, so I'm always trying to get better, I'm always unhappy with myself.

The people in Los Angeles who commissioned the mini-opera ['Under the Volcano'] said they wanted to do it about Malcolm Lowry. I said, 'I know Jack Bruce really well and maybe I could involve Jack in it' and I did. People hear that you're a good composer but very seldom do you get to say, 'I think I'll just write a piece for Sonny Rollins!' Well, Sonny Rollins didn't ask you to write a piece, so you write for who asks you to write. And some weird people have asked me! I always think, 'Oh, damn, I don't want to do this, this is not what I'm into.' But by the time I've finished it I think, 'I'm so glad I was forced to learn what the violin does or about strange percussion instruments.' I feel like James Bond, I know I'm going to be shot at, there'll be awful dangers and I'm going to come out at the end of the book, having succeeded! The real truth is, that about three days after the piece is finished, the thrill is gone and I'm on to the next one.

Angelique Kidjo

© ADRIAN BOOT

Angelique Kidjo grew up in Ouidah, Benin. She was born into a cosmopolitan, artistic family – her mother is a choreographer and theatre director, her brothers are musicians; at the age of six, she was singing and dancing in her mother's theatre company, and later joined her brothers in the Kidjo Brothers Band. Her musical influences ranged from traditional Benin folk songs, to South Africa's Miriam Makeba and that country's urban township music, to western artists like Aretha Franklin, Jimi Hendrix and James Brown. She recorded versions of Makeba's songs for Benin radio, and as her solo success grew, she toured West Africa.

Deciding against pursuing law studies in Benin, she moved to Paris in 1983, to join the community of musicians from Francophone Africa, marrying African musical traditions with western influences to create their own hybrid genre. She studied opera and jazz, and joined the band Pili Pili, going on to record several albums with them and performing at the Montreux jazz festival in 1987. The same year, she joined forces with French bass-player/composer Jean Hebrail, whom she later married. She formed her own band and, in early 1991, released her first solo album, 'Parakou', which mixed traditional African makossa and zouk with soul and reggae rhythms and digital dance mixes. Later that year, she released 'Logozo' which consolidated her growing reputation as the diva of Afro-funk dance music. It also featured a version of the Tanzanian love-song 'Malaika', origi-nally made famous by Miriam Makeba. In 1994, 'Aye', the follow-up album – recorded at Prince's Paisley Park Studios in

Minneapolis, and in Paris and London – was acclaimed as her most sophisticated to date.

Although she speaks fluent French and English, Angelique Kidjo records primarily in her native language, Fon (although she has recorded in other African languages), asserting that the spirit and sentiment of her music will come through her delivery, transcending the need for translation. Her albums and singles have featured on international world music and dance charts, although she has angered some world music purists who object to the dominance of the techno and dance rhythms in her work.

Inspired by the strongly political stand taken by Miriam Makeba in her music, Angelique Kidjo's lyrics frequently address social issues and divisions – calling on African nations to develop strong economic and health systems, challenging the traditional roles of women, highlighting homelessness, poverty and political repression.

Angelique Kidjo lives in Paris with her husband, Jean Hebrail, and their daughter.

In West Africa there is much more the culture of women singing in Mali and Senegal, than in Benin, where mainly the singers are male. When I decided to sing, I did not make up my mind and know that I was going to be a singer, it just happened. It got to the point where I made the first record for the African market in 1980 and with this album, I was touring West Africa, to become known out of Benin.

Now I'm realising how a lot of girl singers in Africa are fighting against society, fighting against the government. And artists can be something precious for the country. Now, I think I am blessed. Now, I can't thank God enough, and my parents enough, for making me the person I am today. I chose music instead of law, because I said to myself, 'The thing I want to do as a lawyer, I can do with my music but touch many more people than being a lawyer.' Because you talk only to an individual, even if you are known all over the world because you defend human rights . . . the satisfaction can never be like music because you have barriers. So I'm happy to be a singer because I'm completely responsible for it.

When I arrived in France, I said to myself 'Here you are!' My parents did not want me to go because they knew that life was difficult there. But the choices were not that many. Because I could either stay in Benin and use my music to praise the revolution or I could leave the country. So I decided to go. It went against [everything] to sing against something I don't believe in. Before I left, I was talking to my parents and they told me, 'Look, we are here to support you. We can't decide for you what you're going to do so you have to make up your mind.'

[In Paris] I was in music school, I was studying classical music and French *variété* so I discovered other singers that I did not know in Benin. For the first time in my life I was singing Verdi and Offenbach and it was very interesting; by singing Verdi or Offenbach I started to discover other things. We used to discuss it and I used to say, 'This is bullshit; there is no rhythm, what kind of music can it be?' And they used to tell me, 'Listen! Don't think about it'. It took me a while, to think, 'Oh, this is Mozart, this is Beethoven, and Chopin' and I started to like it because of the atmosphere . . . and for a musician, classical music is very important for your writing and your composing. So after that school, I went to a jazz school and I decided to be a singer.

I wish all artists knew how you make a hit. Nobody knows; there is no recipe for that. You make your album in your solitude and when the album is ready and out, it doesn't depend on you any more. You can do absolutely nothing to help it. I make my music and I make my albums; that is the point. The rest belongs to the public, I have no hand in it. If people like it, that's OK; if people don't like it, it's OK because that's how life is. I don't know one human being that everybody loves. Even someone who is an angel. We hated Jesus Christ and we killed Jesus Christ and he came to save us, so who am I? I accept completely that it can be that people don't like my music but not liking my music doesn't mean that because you don't like my music you can insult me. That's the only thing that I don't like and I won't let anybody do it. If you criticise my work, it's your job, and you do it right. But not to involve my person – what I am is none of their business.

I can't do something I don't know, which is not in my blood, or which is not in my heart. So simply, I learned from my traditional music how to let people dance first, take out the stress and take the lesson out from that. It is the other way around in the white people's society. If you feel oppressed, you are already stressed, then you feel guilty, and they oppress you still further. In our society, it's not like that. It doesn't matter how heavy, how strong, how painful the song is. First of all, you move your body. Then, after you start to listen to it, you'll move your body even more because you are angry, and you go out and you do something.

Apart from that, you have another part of traditional music of Benin, of the south, where I come from, which is only for the burial ceremony. In those cases, you can cry but generally for a burial ceremony, all the heavy subjects are in the way that you listen to it. My job and my duty is not to make people feel guilty. Who am I? I'm not here to judge anybody. I'm here to say what I think is right for me and if you work with me, you do what you want to change it. That's it.

That's how music has been taught to me. The people in my country listen much more to traditional singers than to politicians, because they [singers] always write about a situation that involves us and the only way to get through it and to get the people into it, is to play music. Even when there is a revolt, the people revolting sing. I was eight years old when I first saw all the population of [my] country standing up and saying, 'No, we don't want that president.' It was warriors singing. They don't have any guns, they don't have anything. They have their singing and they walk to the president, saying 'We don't want that shit.' And the president left. It was very powerful, they didn't need guns.

What I admired first in Miriam Makeba is her courage because her first songs were absolutely against the [South African] government. And perhaps unconsciously somehow, somewhere that counts. I don't think it's just because she was like that, it's because I've been taught by my parents to fight for the truth. And since I was a little girl, I've always fought against injustice. It doesn't matter if it's my business or not, I jump in. I can't stand it. You can kill me but I'll know why I died, and you'll know why you killed me. So, I've always been like that; I never shut my mouth when I know it's the truth. You can be beating me to death, but I'm going to scream it. Sometimes that bothers some people but that's how I am; you take me or you don't take me.

You have two types of racism in Europe and in the world. You have the physical racism and you have the art racism. There was talk a long time ago that Africa didn't have any art, any culture, and nobody wanted to say that Picasso had taken a lot from African art. But the evidence, the truth, you can't hide it; one day it's going to come out. The fact is that the other type of racism we have is due to crisis. When there's a crisis, all of the extremism comes out because the population are fragmented. Extreme people have been always on the ground, taking advantage of the anguish, that's why it can happen. But the thing that's frightening me is that it seems to me that the example of the Second World War with Hitler did not bring any solution to human hatred. I have the impression that all those millions of human beings that were killed during this war gave their lives for nothing.

And it's painful to see how human beings can be sometimes stupid. We are ready to do anything to kill. And after we say that there are wild animals in the jungle, we have to ask ourselves if we are civilised, because for me, we are not. Absolutely not civilised . . . we act like monsters, because the lion kills only when he is hungry; even when we are full, we kill. So who is wild – the lion or the human being? Who is the worst predator between the two of them? I think it's the human being.

There is one thing that human beings can share, without any nationality, race or colour and that's stupidity. Some people think that because some white people come to our country, they don't have the right to use our music. Music is not about white or black. But some white people come and take advantage of black people and make their own money and have great success without giving anything [back]. Do you know one artist who puts the African musician on the same level with him? Peter Gabriel.

But on the other hand, you have some journalists – that's where I'm coming to the racism in art – who don't know anything about Africa. The only thing they know, at least, is from TV. And if they're a little bit more intelligent, from a book. I don't want to be rude but that's how I feel when they address me. Because one of them says, 'What is African in your music?' Some of them will say, 'Do you think you are making African music?' What do they know about it? I'm not going to say to Peter Gabriel, or Mick Jagger, 'Are you making English rock music?' That type of question, I can't even think of. And that is a kind of racism, because those [journalists] say they are purists of music because if you start to talk about purism in music, then you can share the same idea with the neo-Nazis. That's what is scary. They don't even want to dirty music; that I can never accept. That's why, with that type of journalist, I throw them out, I don't want to speak to them and I don't want to see them! Because they're supposed to know better than the Africans, what to do. They're supposed to know our culture better than us. And they are supposed to know what we have to do, and they have to tell us what to do. Sometimes you have the impression that slavery and colonisation are not over. They are still there and there are still people who are ready to put you in a big hole and close you down. And I say, 'No!'

The thing in Paris is that politics and the government

show the open face of racism. Nobody feels ashamed of being a racist. Today, it's a kind of fashion. There is a kind of pride to being a racist. So what are you going to tell the poor guy in the street who is looking at you like a piece of shit when his government gave him the legitimacy to do that. The fact is that when you are a musician you travel a lot. I hear things. But when I first started to come out with my baby some people looked at my baby like they are full of hate – you can see it, you can smell it, you can see it in their eyes. So there is something wrong if you hate a baby, a three-month-old who did not do anything to you but just existed, because the mother is black. It's frightening. So that means anything could happen. There is no solution because the government does not want to be involved. Because all that's been happening in Germany – if the government wanted to stop it, they have the power of stopping it. Most of the riots happened when the [security] forces were there. That is frightening. Because the policemen are there to save people and they did not do that.

I'm not only put in the position of talking only about Africa, for me I have to talk about everybody because what's happening in Africa affects Europe and so on and so on. Here we are living in a world where you can't [separate] Africa from Europe and from the United States, because the crisis is general. So of course I am in a good position to talk about my country and my continent and every time that I have the opportunity, I do. But I aim, too, to talk about what's happening in France, what's happening in the United States and what's happening here [Britain]. I used to say, 'I wish there could be a world citizen's passport because I'm going to have it!' Because all the problems that have something to do with human beings are the same. It's only the importance which is different.

———————————————■———————————————

In Benin, the people know me; I'm their sister, I'm their daughter, I'm everything. What I discovered there is young people have cut their hair like I've cut my hair, and they dress like I dress, and every two weeks they have [a competition for] the best interpretation of Angelique Kidjo, between schools. I did not believe it until I saw it! I went to a club to have a drink and they told me, 'you missed something'. There was a college group here. One of the musicians saw me and grabbed the rest and they came and they set up and they played my songs for me and they played them well! And they told me, 'we dedicate it to you'.

And a lot of artists come to me and tell me, 'Thanks, we understand what you're talking about. You sing in our language; it means something for us.' When I go back home, I say 'Oh boy, what am I doing', but at the same time I'm happy because we consume a lot of music from England, from America, from France, and that gives them an idea that it's always possible. But it's frightening because it's a big responsibility you have. I can't fail and when you're a human being with that type of pressure, you can't take it for long because any human being can fail.

I used to say, 'Speaking French or speaking English is different from writing a song in that language.' The thing, for me, that's important is that if you like languages, that means that you respect the people who speak that language so I can't afford to take the risk of singing in English or French without being very sure of what I'm going to say. If one day I decide to make an album in English or French, I will decide because I've found somebody with whom I can sit down and write those lyrics together that mean something to me. And I can talk about things. That's why I did not do it. My public is very important to me. I'm not singing for myself; I can sing then in my bathroom. I'm singing to touch people's souls. That means respect yourself and respect them. If you fool the public, it's like a child, the child smells it and you can't lie. So, when you make music, you're supposed to talk to human beings, you are obliged in a way to use all the forces, all the languages you can use.

Emotion doesn't need words. The deaf can speak to you, and cry, and you know, even if you don't speak the language. For me, music is a kind of silk that you put around a gift, which is the song. Because the song needs that silk to look very beautiful. And there are different colours of silk around those songs.

Everybody has different characters. I did not cut my hair to look like Grace Jones, it's not a kind of style. It's just because, at a moment in my life, I didn't have time any more to have long hair. I'm not a fashionable person. When I want to wear my hair like this, I will; if I want to grow it, I'll grow it. Nobody can tell me what to do. I don't tell anybody not to cut their hair. I'm not here to fulfil anybody's . . . fantasies. That drives me nuts. Some people when they see African women, they see the breasts out and they think about bed! Apart from that [they think], you have nothing in your mind, you can't think by yourself, and especially, you can't make that kind of music. Excuse me! I can't take that any longer because it's not true.

So this kind of machismo is none of my business. Even if a man doesn't feel himself strong enough to face a woman who has a little bit of character, that means he's nothing. I don't want to waste my time with that type of talk. Those types of people, I don't envy them. I wish for them a long life and for us both to meet when we are both old and we will sum up our life. My life will be much richer than his life.

I would like [my daughter] to live in a world a little bit more equal, less poverty, less jobless and I would like her to be optimistic, to be positive, to be blessed with love. To love herself, because it's going to be tough for her; she has two cultures, to be part of having two cultures; not to let herself be destabilised by anybody. And to live her life; *her* choice will be mine. I'm happy like this, so I think she's going to be happy. But the thing I won't like my baby to be is to be impolite, I can't support that. So she will be taught very early about respect, because if you want people to respect you, you have to respect yourself. That will be one of the things I won't give up.

Jane Siberry

J ane Siberry was born in Etobicoke, Canada, in 1956. She taught herself to play the piano when still very young, and improvised, playing by ear. She moved to Toronto at the age of seventeen, to attend the University of Guelph, to study science. Although much taken with punk music at the time, she opted for the acoustic guitar, teaching herself to play by studying the *Leonard Cohen Songbook*. She began to write her own songs, performing them in Toronto's cafes.

Her self-titled debut album was released on the independent Duke Street Records label in 1981, financed by money she had earned as a waitress. She co-produced the folk-tinged album with David Bradstreet and Carl Keesee. The follow-up, 'No Borders Here', released three years later on Open Air Records, marked the beginning of her co-production partnership with bassist John Switzer. The folk influence receded as synthesisers became a part of her work for the first time and the single, 'Mimi on the Beach', sold well as a result. 'The Speckless Sky' album in 1985 veered into more pop-oriented territory, earning a gold record and two CASBY awards, the Canadian equivalent of the Grammys.

By the time Jane Siberry made her debut on a major American label – Reprise – with 'The Walking' in 1987, her quirky lyrics and increasing confidence in musical experimentation was being favourably compared to those of Laurie Anderson and Joni Mitchell. But the album failed to make a dent in the pop charts or gain significant radio play – not surprising, given that only three of the album's eight tracks ran less than five minutes, and one of them was more than ten.

'Bound by the Beauty', released in 1989, marked significant departures – it was Jane Siberry's first as solo producer, and showed a more improvisational style, with a new group of musicians. While critically acclaimed, its performance, commercially, was fairly lack-lustre – a fan letter from Brian Eno, lamenting this state of affairs, led to a production collaboration between the two on Siberry's sixth album, 'When I Was a Boy'. The album included a duet with k d lang, 'Calling All Angels', which had originally featured on the soundtrack to the Wim Wenders' film, *Until the End of the World*, in 1992. The same year, it was also included on the compilation album of selected tracks from her previous records, 'Summer in the Yukon'.

Her work on film soundtracks also includes Wim Wenders' 1993 film, *Far Away, So Close!* on which she contributed 'Slow Tango', *The Crow* (starring Brandon Lee) and the documentary *Underwater*, for the American Film Institute.

Videos released for tracks on 'When I Was a Boy' showed Siberry's growing involvement with and interest in the visual medium – she produced several video pieces to accompany her performances after the release of the album. These appearances also marked a departure for her, becoming as much a showing of her video work, or a presentation of her spoken word pieces as a musical improvisation session. She would also take questions from the audience.

Jane Siberry lives in Toronto, Canada.

As a child, I would only play [the piano] when my family was out of the house. Things made sense when I played music and it was the one thing I trusted, so I would play. But I found that to be interrupted when I was playing – because I only improvised when I was young – was too much of a shock to my system; when someone would come in and ask me a question, then I would feel too vulnerable. They would interrupt me, and it would startle me. On-stage, it's deliberate and you understand the situation. It's not like you're totally open and playing and someone barges into the room and you have a heart attack! So I became a closet family musician who never played in front of them.

When I started playing in public when I was about seventeen I was just so used to sort of 'blowing' on piano, as soon as I had to be conscious of it on-stage, I just couldn't make the leap, so people would be very curious, because I sounded like I could hardly play piano – although I could, not too badly. I would play songs that I had written; I started to write when I was sixteen. I could play guitar, but piano's always been my first breath. I trust the piano, and I look to the piano to tell me how I'm feeling, because often I won't know until I sit down. And I'll go, 'Oh, I had no idea I was feeling like that!'

I used [music] as a medicine, a self-medicine. It would be a way to hear myself and a way to balance myself because I'd start playing and . . . then the music would change into something else. People are so wise; people know how to take care of themselves, especially children. You play and then you go into this kind of music instinctively; you can't even be conscious of it. I can't even be conscious of it now to describe it; much more is going on than we have tools to understand . . . Until finally, the right point came to stop. The medicine had run its course.

I see now that I was very sensitive and really wanted love, and was impressionable. It doesn't sound any different from anyone else, does it? It's not different from anyone else . . . just living in a typically spiritually arid environment, I learned not to be so sensitive. So I shut down and I lost my voice, sort of physically. I rarely speak without tension in my voice, and you become aware of it as a singer because you need to tune in to where you want to go and you find you can't get there when you want to and then you have to figure out why.

I lost my voice on a metaphysical level too, in that I made the decision that saying what was on my mind would remove love from my environment. Which is what everyone learns.

You're just quickly taught not to be too loud, not to be too extreme on any level, not to be angry, not to express anger; certain things are allowed, a certain amount of sadness but that's our culture. And that gave me a series of earaches that I've had since I was young, which actually turned out to be jaw spasms, a locked jaw. And I do believe the mind and body are connected. And I started to notice that when I was not speaking my truth I would go into these spasms until finally, they would make me cry, the pain would be so bad. So finally, I had to leave the room and I couldn't release it unless I cried. And I started to understand the voice on a different level, about speaking your truth and not hating myself so much for not being able to . . . for hearing how much tension there was in my voice. I see it now as something I designed for myself to learn what I wanted to learn and sing in more of an interested way than a critical way.

Five years ago, I would have said, 'I never expected little old me to be on the other side of the audience, or to be successful in this way.' And now, I say 'part of me knew it all along' but I would always dismiss that absolute knowing as arrogance. But now I see that everyone has it, and you have to be so fast because it's in the first millisecond of when you ask a question to yourself, or when someone asks you a question, the very first millisecond of your response is your truth. And after that the mind kicks in. You have to be fast, don't you? Often you think it's arrogance. Or someone says, 'Oh, my father died'. I used to think I was different than everyone because I would notice; I'd say, 'yes', I wouldn't go 'oh'. My first thought was emotion-free; it was fact and that it's totally fine that he died and that includes all the pain and everything that goes with it. I didn't understand that that was acceptable and I thought it was because I was a terrible person. That's a good example of how I saw the world and now it's quite different and much healthier and I'm much happier and I know that my way of seeing all of this is right because I have way more energy. Every now and then I move into states of fearlessness which equals freedom, which equals the way we're supposed to walk this earth.

------------------------■------------------------

Other cultures have rites of initiation into maturity, into adult-hood, they send you out in a raft or you're out in the forest for three days with no food or water, to find your own mettle. But we don't have it in our culture, there is very little consciousness of working on that level of yourself. I was in a situation where I felt I had reached the bottom of something and I had nothing to lose. The things I cared most about, like the music I write, and sending it out, reaching people, all these things I felt I had nothing to lose, I felt it was all a failure. And it was at that moment, all of a sudden, that I felt more free than I had ever felt. I hope I always remember that state of nothing-to-lose equals freedom. Because that's when you can finally, without consideration of anything else, hear what you really want to do and what you really believe in and what really will make you – as you teeter on the smoking rubble at the end of your life – be able to say, 'Yes!'

Who knows how long I had been putting off things I hadn't faced. I'd been on the treadmill for about eight or nine years without feeling like I had done everything I had to do. And finally, I was able to go under, so to speak, for two or three months at a time, long periods of time, without having to func-tion normally and during those times I would trust myself ultimately to do what I had to do. I listened to my body; if I felt I had to do this or that, I would. It's like being in love or being afraid for your life when you hear someone climbing up your stairs or whatever. I think it's important to hear that other human beings are going through the same things you are.

As things would come to consciousness, instead of hating myself for all of the things that I thought made me dark and dull and heavy, I started to understand and I went back through the root of looking at the beginning of my life and seeing how

I'd made certain decisions and the whole anger thing against [my] family and the hurt, even though part of me still understood that it had to happen that way and . . . you can't go from trauma to compassion without the in-between stage of feeling it. I didn't even know half the time what was going on but fortunately I trusted myself so I would just lock the door and become totally soggy for two weeks at a time and do my own therapy so to speak, or just listen to myself and not have time to do that. And that was a gift.

The completion of ['When I Was a Boy'] came from that place – a good solid, stubborn place of saying, 'I have to be creative every day and I won't ask anyone's permission and I won't ask for money.' So I started taking hold of my creative activities again, because often I would have ideas or I'd like to do this or that but then someone would say, 'No, you can't do your own video because we do it', then they don't do it because you're small potatoes so you end up doing nothing. So I went back into that very healthy state and independent street-style of doing things really cheaply; of taking my power back into my own hands. To go back to where I was when I first was free – you have an idea and you do it. You never have anyone to ask. I think my [video] stuff is much more undiluted than the stuff I've done through the record company and other directors, and people who are really too busy to do their homework or become familiar with your work, or they're just sort of wanking on their own spectrum of styles.

A lot of the lessons I've learned over the last three years is that every time I said 'You do it, you must know better than me', it would backfire and I'd end up with work that wasn't right. So I'd have to re-do things and they'd cost more money and I'd have to ask for things. And so I realised that was something I was being shown again and again . . . to finally own that I actually am a really good producer and a really good writer and arranger in spite of a lot of feedback that I was a problem child, and just a burden on the record company, and I just made things difficult and they wanted to help me but if I kept writing songs that weren't singles . . . !

And now I say 'If I can only be open, I'll do an amazing job myself' and I think the quality of the work has gone up with that attitude. Ever since I signed any kind of record deal, I knew that the only way that I would do well was to do things my way, and that even if they brought someone in and did it their way, it might do better in the short-term but not ultimately. The only way I would do well was to trust myself and then the result would be the strongest it could be. So, every time I didn't trust myself, I would be shown that. So I made a commitment, I said, 'OK then, since I'm at the bottom and I have nothing to lose, I'm going to commit myself one hundred per cent to trusting my instinct and I'm going to try it and just see how it goes.' Blind faith! Something that I couldn't really understand deep down, but I was going to try it. Every question I'm asked, I run it through that, how I feel. 'Will you tour?', they mean with a band; [I feel] I'm not supposed to. 'Oh no!' and then those voices start again: 'But we put all this money into your record and we've done this and that, and you're once again sabotaging it, deliberately working against what you want.' And I have to say, 'I'm trying to trust that if I listen to myself, I will get what I want.' And now, it's sort of sinking in.

I think of the story of Peter, Jesus and the Apostles so often because I don't understand how someone could walk out on the water, to have that much faith. The day that ['When I Was a Boy'] was released in England, I was sitting in the lobby of the hotel and I heard my music playing, and I went up to the [Reception] Desk and said, 'Where did you get that?' because no one's heard of me there unless they're sort of underground and finally they called upstairs to try to figure it out and they said, 'Some guy who works here brought it in.'

So I went back and sat down and a few minutes later he walks up to me and he says, 'I got an advance copy last night and I went home and listened to it in my living-room and when I was listening to it, I saw you sitting here in the lobby, and I knew you'd be here.' And then I left and I went up to St Patrick's church just to light a candle for the record and just as I walked in, he [the priest] started reading about the boat, people walking out and having faith. Every decision I make, I try to say, 'Is that coming from faith or is that coming from fear?'

In record companies, the people who sign you aren't the people who market you. That's a whole different department. It's hard work. And also the creative people are doing music and not necessarily promoting it. And to promote something that doesn't fit into the normal machine takes creative thinking, so my manager and I are always coming up with different things. I decided that, rather than be frustrated, I'll just create a way to reach the people who are interested and then I can keep doing tons of little projects that keep me happy.

But the pressure's there. In my case, it's sort of insidious, it comes from me. It's not from the [record company] saying, 'we need singles', so much. It's more than that. It would be easier for me if I thought they were all assholes and hated them. I have to feel free enough to really hear what I want to do but I run that funny line of actually feeling respected by a lot of people in the record company and that the music-lover in them really does want to put their energy into helping my music reach more people. So my heart sort of gets a bit open and then you sort of wish it wasn't so hard for people that you like because you know it's frustrating for them. So it's insidious and it tricks me and then I worry about having their love withdrawn and then I get weak again.

Certain women have a fear of creative energy; some women are more masculine that way. And I think everyone has both energies; and some women are more rigid than men. They're just more doers, they're not connected to that sort of bubbly flowing energy that is creativity and femininity and giddiness of life or whatever you want to call it. I feel most vulnerable on-stage when I can't find that female energy in me. When I can't find that funny bubbling feeling that will flow, which is how I function. And that's how I write.

I was doing an interview with someone from England when ['When I Was a Boy'] first came out and they were talking about the difference between it and my other records, saying it couldn't be considered an ethereal record, in the way that my other ones had been, because there was a physical connection in it that came through the voice and it came through the choice of rhythms. And that also, I couldn't be called a female singer-songwriter and I kept saying, 'Why not? Why not?' And I think it's because there's an innate truth, a ferret-, weasel-like wisdom within the inarticulate listener that recognises balance or not, and that there is a bit of truth to the female singer-songwriter. Maybe people are using the wrong words, but often there is just perhaps, a certain, what's called 'ballsiness' that would make it hard to call someone a female singer-songwriter. That's what seems to tip the scale, in order to lose the word 'female'. And so the lumping together; often, there's something to look at in any casual, careless, lazy lumping. Often, there's a certain wisdom to it.

As far as comparisons, I use them all the time. Any writer does; it's a way of communicating information. It's the most accurate way to draw a picture for someone, but often they're lazy and very superficial and then you start to recognise good writers and lazy writers. And the good writers come up with more unusual comparisons but they really are comparing more essential qualities than whether you all have high cheekbones or you're blonde or have a crack in your voice.

I'm much more appreciative and not afraid to like women's work and I actually was on tour with only men, on the last tour, and I was sitting in a restaurant, and I was always with men, and I got so lonely because I couldn't speak a certain way. That tour really made me appreciate what is so beautiful about women, you speak and you sense a resonance, a depth. And with certain men, you just don't even bother saying anything . . . isn't that a curious thing? Not all men, of course, and not all women, but I was in a restaurant and I was sitting there, and I thought 'I feel something very strange' and I looked around and it was the woman behind me at the next table. I was just feeling a woman's energy behind me. It was so black and white, so clear, it was like a sweet perfume, but it wasn't perfume. It really made me see that.

I used to actually sense an imbalance in the whole women thing. It was just an animal instinct and I would really actually turn away from anything that felt too women-oriented, but that was coming from who I was then and as I started to grow, now I've come to a) love children, which I never did, and b) love women. I found children very uninteresting and I didn't like the way people revered them. That wasn't quite right because everyone was a child once and those children were going to be boring adults one day so what was the big deal! And I had no memories of myself as a nice child or a sweet child. I only thought I was a nothing child, and any picture I looked at, of myself, I only saw that the light was gone, that I looked vacant. That's how I felt as a child – I turned off quickly, very obedient, to get approval. I was very obedient and sensitive so I turned off my sensitivity . . . and then hoped to get more love and approval. Our culture is very disrespectful towards the innate wisdom and nobility of the human being. From the moment you're born, it's assumed that someone else knows better than you, knows when you're hungry more than when you know you're hungry.

[Many performers feel] that if there isn't separation, then there won't be any mystery any more and you won't be accorded the respect you deserve. And yet I've always felt that people are endlessly mysterious and the more you get down to who they really are, the more the window widens. It's like a big mirror, they're seeing themselves through me and there is a common experience and they could never hear what I say unless they'd felt it themselves.

Music is very intimate; that's one of the great things about it. I used to live across from a mental health centre. To me, that could be a metaphor for a song that speaks for you, and you say thank you . . . it wasn't a song, it was all day, every day, unfiltered humanity speaking out and sometimes there'd be lots of 'fuck', and anger and lots of absolute ecstasy. All sorts of emotions and so often, I felt like they'd spoken for me. I would have to say 'thank you' up in my little kitchen. I feel that way but you said it for me, so thanks!

I feel it's partly my job to create words, or become an articulator of things that are difficult to articulate because then it does expand the language. It gives you a more precise way to describe how you're feeling. I like the idea of fragments, just caught. I like the idea of a sense of 'caughtness' because then you get a sense of a 'before' and an 'after', so you only have to say a little bit and the rest is inherent around it. I like titles like 'Row, row, row your boat'; I was going to call one album [that]. That's all you have to say, and everyone, in their mind, traces the rest of the line and it's such a beautiful line, 'gently down the stream, merrily, merrily, merrily, life is but a dream'. I like things like that because they're so open, the listener can expand as wide as they like. In discussing these things, that's not why I do them consciously, but there's a sense of that unconsciously.

I almost stayed in my old habit of being a fence-sitter, or defusing anything that I felt was too polarised, not using images that would date me, I don't mean age-wise, but that would make the song less meaningful twenty years from now and I knew angels were very attractive right now. They're in the air, just like the word 'abuse', 'dysfunctional', the buzzwords – even the word, 'buzzword'. There's a truth to them, there's a reason they're in the air. They're filling us up and then they'll leave. And the 'angel' thing. All these things are important and then people react against them, and then you find them on coffee mugs and it trivialises them. I almost controlled what I was putting out, but I didn't this time. I said I didn't want to be linked with angels particularly, but I just won't control it. But I have always been very reverent, [with a] very devotional nature towards Nature. I kneel before the altar of beauty in any form; it could be a tree, or an office tower. But if you find beauty in it, that's my God.

———————————————◼———————————————

Improvisation is not a big part of the pop world but it's part of my life and so desperate am I to do that sometimes, that I've been known to go to karaoke bars and pick some songs I don't know and then improvise with the words, but it really pisses people off, it doesn't go over big. They want you to sing it the right way; they get really upset . . . so there's all this energy coming at you to guide you to the right note! The improvisation is the most exciting thing about music and it does take a lot of trust and for some reason, much as I feel I'm just slowly finding my voice again, and have done all sorts of screwy things to myself, I've always trusted musically, so that's been like a saving grace.

I'm disciplined enough to create a time space to be free in, when I know it's time to do a new record, but I go with inspiration mostly. When I have to work nine-to-five every day, I get angry. Say, I'm in the studio; structured time starts to make me pissed off and I'm much better just going with how I'm feeling. The reason it pisses me off is because I become anxious and worried that I won't be able to do it within that time, the pressure, but that's all in my own mind so that's something just to look at. And then you go into that state of trust and say, 'Whatever happens will be just fine' and sort of put yourself in a trusting place. So it's not that I want to do without discipline, it's that I want to do without the worry. But what I do takes a lot of structuring and discipline, and in the writing I'm very disciplined about sorting the wheat from the chaff, keeping stuff that I consider inspired as opposed to the stuff that comes from being clever.

———————————————◼———————————————

When I do a song for a film track, or just go and sing back-up vocals for someone, I can do it quickly and there's a different set of sensors. It allows me to follow a different Muse, different than I would when I put out a record, which is a 'whole' thing. I like to do bits and pieces too, because there's a different freedom that I feel. I did another thing for Wim Wenders, his sequel to *Wings of Desire.* But [the record company] didn't feel that I could be on the soundtrack for the film because I wasn't well enough known. So they felt that if k d [lang] sang on it, they could have 'Calling All Angels' on it. And that's just stuff that goes on. I knew her already but we had never sung together. I hadn't finished singing it myself, I hadn't finished rewriting the lyrics. I changed them, it used to be a sort of 'hurtin' country song about a man I was lusting after. So k d came in, and we were in different booths singing together, but it wasn't quite connecting. So we came out of the booths and set ourselves up close together so we could see each other, and so there was not a sound barrier between us. And then we sang. I think most musicians will say how important this is, to physically be near to someone, like close on-stage; it's really important. And then we did that singer-ly thing, and connected; we were able to look into each other's eyes and it felt really great. And she just immediately improvised which not everyone does. And then about two weeks after that, my vibrato, my diaphragm loosened. I swear, somehow osmotically, my being said, 'It is right and healthy to learn how to finally relax a bit more when you sing.' And I received this information from being close to her. And also my vibrato started changing; sometimes it was so wild and out of control that I'd start to get seasick!

This has to do partly with thinking about why you're doing this book and why I think it's great. I do feel that, at this time of the earth's history, at a critical point, if it is to be healed, it's going to come from women's energy, whether it's women's energy in men or women. Just from that kind of energy. And that's why it's so important that all the resonance that we feel when we speak to women is there for a reason. It's a gift, it's a sensitivity that's going to finally be called into action, instead of put down, because then you're working with all the cables attached, to do what's going to be necessary to turn things around. And anything that strengthens that – like what you're doing with this book – any time you see that you have to say, 'yes, yes, yes', you have my total support!

It's women's energy in balance with male energy; it has to be the mixture. The male energy is the 'doing' energy, the female energy is the wisdom, but it has to be a mixture of both. But women will know how to bring things into balance. It's not just women's energy, it's women's ability to bring things into balance.

Monie Love

© EDDIE MONSOON/COURTESY COOLTEMPO

M onie Love (Simone Johnson) was born in London in 1970. As a child she travelled between New York, where her mother was living, and London, where her father had his home. She began to write poetry and got involved in the US musical import of the early-'80s, hip hop. She and her friends would go to London's Covent Garden market where, among the street performers who gathered there, they'd join the break-dancers, dancing to a hip hop beat.

Inspired, first by her parents' reggae records, and then by the late-'70s funk-soul stars, she devised her own version of the rap music which followed hip hop. While rapping in clubs, she made two singles which were released by small independent labels but these failed to have any commercial impact. They did bring her to the attention of Cooltempo, the dance label of Chrysalis Records.

Fine Young Cannibals invited her to rap on the extended mix of their British Top Ten (and US Number One) song, 'She Drives Me Crazy'. Monie Love moved to New York to record her debut album, on which Fine Young Cannibals' David Steele and Andy Cox co-wrote and co-produced three tracks. Other guests featured on the heavily dance-influenced album included hip hop stars The Jungle Brothers and Afrika Baby Bambaataa.

In New York, she was embraced by the Afro-centric group-ing of artists, Native Tongues, which evolved as a counter-movement to the hard-core gangsta rap with its images of violence and misogyny. She performed and recorded with several of the groups including De La Soul, Tribe Called Quest,

Almond Joy and The Jungle Brothers. The most high-profile of these was her guest appearance on Queen Latifah's single, 'Ladies First', a strong woman-oriented response to the excesses of the hard-core rappers. She also performed on Almond Joy's 'Back to the Black', a song denouncing the use of hair extensions and make-up among young black women.

Her own album, 'Down to Earth', released in 1990, picked up on such themes in songs like 'Race Against Reality', but it also contained unadulterated dance-floor hits like 'It's a Shame', 'Monie in the Middle' and 'Grandpa's Party', a tribute to the legendary godfather of hip hop, Afrika Bambaataa. Three years later, the follow-up album 'In A Word or 2' was musically more focused, with lyrics which reflected the growing social awareness she felt following the birth of her daughter, Charlena.

When she was told that Prince wanted to work with her on the album, she thought it was a joke; an invitation to his Paisley Park studios in Minneapolis proved her wrong. He co-produced three tracks, including 'Born 2 BREED', as much an allusion to her new-found status as a mother, as a call for understanding of the problems facing young parents and their children.

Between albums, Love branched into acting, making her debut, with her baby daughter, in *Strapped*, directed by the actor Forest Whitaker. She had earlier been chosen for a role in Spike Lee's film *Jungle Fever*, but had to cancel her appearance when she discovered that she was pregnant; the role went to Queen Latifah. And she appeared in *Who's the Man*, which featured a galaxy of rap stars including Ice-T, Dr Dre and Ed Lover. Her television work included hosting a game show for MTV.

Monie Love lives in New York with her husband and their daughter.

I grew up on Bob Marley; that wasn't a choice, that was my parents' thing. That was my parents' salvation: Bob Marley, Peter Tosh, Bunny Wailer, all the old reggae artists. That was cool, I got used to it. My choice was Sister Sledge, Kool and the

Gang, Chic, all the early-'70s funk-soul music, that was what powered me along to do whatever I had to get done. I wanted to expand my horizons, but I didn't know how or with what. I didn't know I wanted to be in the music industry but I knew that I appreciated music and I loved to listen to music, and everything to do with my life had to do with music.

I had chores every weekend; my mother said I could do whatever I wanted to do as long as I did my chores. So I would start doing them from Friday so that when I got up on Saturday, the majority of my day wouldn't be wasted on chores. I did them already! I used to play music to clean the bathtub, clean the floor, and clean the sink and dust the furniture. I used to have music blasting, music used to help me get through everything.

I had been writing poetry my whole life in the form of little things that you put in greeting cards; I'd make little greeting cards and write poems in them and give them to different family members. Then, I started writing longer poems and printing them in school magazines and taking part in poetry competitions. At the same time, a new wave in England started happening, which was the break-dancing thing. I was into that; I started going to . . . doing my chores on Saturday and going to Covent Garden, where all the street dancers used to be out body-popping and break-dancing and I used to be around there. I used to take part in it, though I never used to spin on my head! Then, the break-dancing and the body-popping ceased, and more DJ-ing started in England, as a chain reaction from movies from the United States. Through watching these movies, I was thinking, 'These girls are saying stuff to music, these guys are saying stuff to music, what is it they're saying? Basically, rhyme, hence, poetry. I write poetry!' So, I thought, what would it sound like if I tried to put what I write to music and I started doing that in the house.

I was thirteen when I started rapping around the house, I'd have my radio on or put a tape in and as I was doing the dishes or whatever, I'd be saying the stuff that I was writing. I didn't get the courage to come out of the house with it until '86 or '87, then I decided to go out into the clubs with it. I let certain friends at school know I could do it and they always asked me to do it at lunch-time and then at Covent Garden, they used to ask me to do it, and there'd be parties where people could get on the microphone and rap and they'd say, 'why don't you come?' Everybody guided me into that avenue.

The whole reason why I got found and signed was because [record company] scouts used to go around to parties and see what the local talent was like. I got found one night when I was working in a club; I said, 'So, you work for a record company; sure, I believe you!' But I gave him my number anyway and sure enough, he did call. And it *was* a record company and they *were* interested in me. I wasn't thinking, 'he likes the look of me' because at that point, I didn't even start thinking about boys in that way until I was about eighteen. I dressed like a boy, I cut all my hair off like a boy, I wore baggy clothes like a boy so I never thought 'that was a line, because he liked the look of me' because there was nothing to see! You couldn't see any type of dimensional shape, because I was completely covered, had my hair cut short, had a baseball cap on and no make-up, no ear-rings.

There's a lot of subliminal things that probably helped mould me into a person who didn't sell out herself to drugs and stuff like that. Thinking about it now, that probably did help my self-esteem when I was sixteen or seventeen years old, that I got recognised for what I did and not for any other superficial reason.

Talking now about the people that I was around when I was younger is ninety-nine per cent of a depressing topic! When I go back to England and I try to touch base with the people that I used to be with, it's really depressing. Other people that are the same age as me are going crazy, like actually, 'assign me to a mental institution!' And I don't understand this, I go back and all these young people are going crazy and doing these desperate things and coked-out. Is it that bad?

I find it hard to comprehend how people that I know, that I went to school with or hung around with as a teenager, could turn their lives into such a nightmare. Nobody could say to me, 'well, you were lucky'. That's bullshit! I wasn't born with a silver spoon in my mouth or anything like that. I was born in the same housing complex as all these other people who were my peers, grew up in the same area, had pretty much the same degree of nice things as anyone else, our clothing was on the same level. I never was ten steps ahead of anybody else when I was growing up. That's why, to a certain extent, I find it difficult to understand when I go back and see these people are crazy or doing drugs. I find it hard to comprehend because I'm not doing any of that! So why should any of them be doing any of that?

I really feel that even if I stayed in England I would not have been like those people. I don't think I'm over-rating myself. I just wouldn't have let it happen. I was fourteen years old when I went out and tried to get my first job in a shoe-store; I lied about my age because I wanted it so badly. I worked for two weeks before they found out how old I was and I got fired because I was too young. I came home and cried my eyes out. My mother said, 'Why are you crying, it's no big deal, Simone, you shouldn't really have been working; it's not like you need to work, you're fourteen years old!'

So I waited for a year until I was fifteen and then I got a job in Burger King for six weeks. After six weeks, I told the boss to take his Whoppers and stick 'em where the sun doesn't shine! I didn't like how he spoke to his workers, not just me. Before he even opened his mouth and said anything to me, I'd see him talking to other members of the staff and he'd be completely outrageously, unnecessarily rude. I just walked out. I was only fifteen years old, but because of the type of upbringing that I had, to this day, if an old person on the street said something really nasty and rude, I would just say to them, 'You don't have to talk to me like that; I understand your dispute but you don't have to speak to me like that.' With my upbringing, I was brought up to respect a person's self-respect.

I've seen people come out now who come from nowhere and escalate to the top and they behave ridiculously, they're real ego-maniacs. I always ask myself the question, 'Why didn't I act like that, why am I still just a regular person?' I think it's because I didn't need the spotlight to know who I was, I didn't need the spotlight for anything. Anything that happened to me after I got in the spotlight, happened to me before.

I took things pretty much in my stride, the whole thing. I never got my hopes up and I still don't. It's like, 'OK, that's cool; if it happens, it happens, if it doesn't, it doesn't.' I'm already preparing myself for if it doesn't. Not in a down way, but my attitude is, 'That's a nice idea that they're throwing at me, if it works out that's cool, but if it doesn't I've still got my job!'

At the time, I liked ['Down to Earth'] but later on I looked back and thought, 'It was OK, it wasn't as fantastic as I thought it was at the time.' It was good enough and it got the job done but I guess it's because as you get older your taste in music changes and grows. What I didn't understand then, but I understand now, was that I was growing musically.

From the first to the second album, I got married, I had a baby. It was scary at that instant, because I was thinking, 'Oh my God, what type of a world is this, that I just brought a child into?' The second album ['In a Word or 2'] was flooded with messages like how this world can be changed and things like that. I lost track of the music itself, I lost track of why I'm a fan of music, what I like to listen to. I was just filled with, 'What can we do to make things better?'

That wasn't what I developed a fan-base for so that album was a bit too far over people's heads, even over mine! I've caught the grip of the music again, and I'm not going to lose the grip of it. It's all part of growing. I never really took part in creating the music and now I've started doing it. It's something that I'm more comfortable with now, and it's the first time that I've really been taking part in it.

I've just gone back to what I love in music. I've just basically said to myself, 'life goes on'. I do still worry about things but to a certain extent I shouldn't because I'd spend more time worrying than getting on and living life. I'm pretty much the same person I was before I had my daughter. With the exception of 'Yes, I'm Mom, and I have to be a trifle more responsible!' but it doesn't mean that I have to be a crone.

'Born 2 BREED' was an abbreviation of Build Relationships where Education and Enlightenment Dominate, basically those being things that I want to instil in Charlena, my daughter. It was about what I wanted to do with my child, and I made it into a song and was trying to say that people should do that with their kids too.

Prince basically contradicted everything that people have ever said about him: 'He's strange, he's secluded, he doesn't speak, he has somebody else speak to you!' None of that happened, he spoke to me, it wasn't even like I was working with Prince, he was just like a normal person! He'd say, 'Have you eaten? Do you want something to eat?' He was so normal that I found it *abnormal*!

---------------------------------■-----------------------------------

As a role model, if that's what people want to call me, I would then say, 'If I'm your role model, then I suggest that you make your own decisions, and follow your own mind and follow your own trials and errors, and not somebody who's on TV or on the radio. Be your own woman.' I never followed any role models. There were people that I liked and admired and looked up to, which is the characteristic of a role model, but I always distinguished the difference between their life and mine. Admire somebody else, appreciate somebody else but create your own life.

I don't think anyone has the right to really ask anyone to be a role model. If it's subliminally appointed to them that they are one, that's fine, then keep it subliminal. But I don't think anybody has a right because that's invading somebody, even though they're a person that's on TV and everyone sees them, or they're on the radio. That's invading their private life, the type of life that you don't see on the TV, which everybody has. That individual has to understand that they are a person within themselves. But to be purposely outwardly appointed as a role model, I don't think anyone has the right to do that.

It was a plus to come out to the United States, considering the line of music that I'm in. And you see that there's something else, other than what you've been seeing, which is England. Making it over here was not an easy task, it wasn't tremendously hard for me either, but I've seen other people try to make it and they've just been completely shut out. I didn't have a hard time because I was lucky that I got embraced by certain people who had a very good profile. It served the purpose of an introduction. The good thing about it is that I didn't press to be on anybody's record; everybody genuinely wanted me to. People liked something about what I was doing. Otherwise, regardless of what set of people I was in with, they would not have accepted me.

I have fun working with people that I like, and things come quickly if I'm working with people that I like. With Latifah, the 'Ladies First' thing was a lot of fun, I was totally into that. We always hung out with each other anyway. It was friendship, 'Let's do this!' We finished it so quickly because we were having so much fun.

When I go back [to England] and I'm just walking around, people in general pat me on the back. But as for the others . . . don't be sore at me because I did something for myself. I'm not going to stay and live in a situation where I cannot excel, simply for a bunch of people that I don't know or care about. Give me a break! The entire rap population throughout the United States, whether they like my music or not, know who Monie Love is. That is the point, regardless of whether they buy my records or not, they all know who I am. I don't see anybody else following me from England!

Nine times out of ten, people seem to like and follow and get with other people from their neighbourhood who made it.

A lot of the harder rappers come out of the harder sections of town so the kids in those sections of town look up to those rappers because they came from their home town. So they eventually fall into whatever it is that artist is saying. [Hard core rap] is going to be there because it does exist, but we don't have to focus ninety per cent of our time on it, there are other genres also.

It's up to women to set themselves apart. Let's not forget that there are sluts in this world! I've met and I've seen them. It's up to each individual woman to set herself apart from the hookers, the sluts and the bitches of the world. And at the same time it's up to the men to set themselves apart from the bitches of the world too, because there are *male* bitches as well.

Follow your heart, whatever is in your heart to do, and completely disregard side-tracking. It's really hard because you'll be doing what you're doing and you'll turn on the TV and see people doing other forms of music and think, 'Well, maybe if I did that, because they're selling platinum' but don't get side-tracked into what somebody else is doing because that can really be your life and death in one blow!

Tanita Tikaram

Tanita Tikaram was born in Munster, Germany, in 1969. Her Fijian father was stationed there with the British Army; her mother is Malayan. The family lived in Germany until Tanita was twelve, then moved to England, settling in Basingstoke, where Tanita was educated. She began writing songs while still at school, and eventually did a showcase at the Mean Fiddler club in London. There she was seen by agent Paul Charles, who later became her manager. Her influences at the time were as much 'West Side Story', Joni Mitchell and Leonard Cohen as Virginia Woolf. Opting for a recording contract with WEA in early 1988, the eighteen-year-old Tikaram's first single, 'Good Tradition', was released in July of that year, and was in the British Top Ten the following month.

An appearance at the Cambridge Folk festival was followed soon after by the release of her first album, 'Ancient Heart' (produced by Peter van Hooke and Rod Argent), which went on to sell three and a half million copies worldwide. A prolific period of creativity followed – most of the songs for her follow-up album, 'The Sweet Keeper', were written while touring to promote 'Ancient Heart'. 'The Sweet Keeper' (also produced by van Hooke and Argent) was released in 1990, followed a year later by 'Everybody's Angel' (co-produced by Tikaram, van Hooke and Argent), which was written in just four weeks. The 1992 release, 'Eleven Kinds of Loneliness', was Tikaram's first solo production, and paid homage to the styles of some of her favourite artists – Nina Simone, Phil Spector, The Beatles and

211

Ry Cooder. And three years later, the album 'Lovers in the City' capitalised on these and her other diverse influences.

Tanita Tikaram lives in London.

———————————————■———————————————

I always thought I was a bit different. Even teachers would say it. It was more my name, people were always going on about my name! Mum made it [Tanita] up. When I was growing up, everybody was moving around a lot but when I went to Basingstoke, it was the big shock of my life because I thought people were quite mobile but most of the children [I met] had never been out of Basingstoke or they hadn't travelled. And I still find that strange. I think my brother became a chameleon and I became known as very bookish. I think when I went to England, I really started reading because I really needed a lot of words. And I couldn't fit in. I just didn't say the right things or I had different references; I couldn't talk about the same things. I've always, even at a very young age, been aware that people are prepared to accept less, you can even see that in kids which is sad.

I had a fantastic childhood, in as much as my brother and I were always making up plays and making up songs, and were always allowed to play. We didn't have a television until we were about ten or eleven because you could only watch German television, and we couldn't understand it so we used to spend all day outside. So when I came to England, I didn't really share the same enthusiasms. I guess everyone was getting into their adolescence and that kind of thing. I can't go back to Basingstoke a lot now, because it's so strange to me. My parents still live there. I'm just overcome by this feeling, I'm sure if I'd stayed there and said 'I want to grow up and be a songwriter', that people would laugh. It's that sort of mentality, where things were so limited. And I think when you're a child, things aren't limited, that's the whole point of being a child. And I always get that feeling there are lots of towns like Basingstoke. It isn't sad, it's just that you don't fit in.

When I was very young, my father used to hang out with Fijians, because he is Indian Fijian and they always had these parties, and they are very tolerant of children, it's not a culture where children have to go to bed, and we used to listen. They all used to start singing songs about their homeland; they were beautiful melodies, and they were quite tragic songs. I just remember watching them, my brother and I would go and get a guitar and start singing and we used to record each other. My brother would do an Elvis impression, and I had to do the backing vocals, so I was kind of a passenger most of the time, following my brother who was much more extrovert. I can remember also loving the songs, The Beatles, a lot of soul, and country music with all these great tragic songs, these straight to the heart songs, my mother was very much into that. There was a whole spate of women singers through the '70s like Anne Murray, Linda Ronstadt, Rita Coolidge, Crystal Gayle, all those sort of singers as well, but people forget them.

My mother had had a child when she was eighteen – my brother – and always said that you should have choices as a woman, not in any grand feminist manner, but 'You should always be independent', and that didn't mean go off and be an artist or something, but you should never have to rely on anyone, you should never let anyone tell you what to do, just do it. I watched her, I had a very close relationship with her. She used to sing when she was young as well. She always said, 'I pushed my children that way [the arts], so they'd have their own freedom.' My brother is an actor. It was always a magical freedom to be an artist, just the idea of it.

I went to a guitar club at school. We used to play 'Lord of the Dance' and things like that, A-A-C-C . . . that was quite funny, but I think that was fine for learning song structure, I always think I learned that from a very young age, I don't know where it comes from now because I certainly don't think about it. I don't think I was particularly focused. I can remember a phase where I thought it was embarrassing that I did music, and so I started acting, only because you got privileges if you did acting, you got time off to rehearse. Supposedly, the most interesting people would do acting but that's not true. I don't think I had best friends, because I can remember a time when I tried to have a best friend, because it was almost a convention at school, you had to have a best friend, otherwise you were really an alien. I didn't and I felt really hopeless.

———————————————■———————————————

I was doing my A levels and then I started writing and I wrote lots of songs very quickly. I think the first song I wrote was 'Poor Cow' and then they just tumbled out, so maybe all these songs were just hiding inside me. I hadn't applied for university, I think because I felt I was going to fail my A levels but I didn't fail them. So I had a year to do something, like earn money or whatever, and I started working in London selling advertising and then I thought, 'OK, I'll try and do music' but my mother said, 'If you can get a record contract in the year, I'll let you go and become a singer' and I said, 'OK, that sounds fair enough'. In my innocence, I thought, 'OK, I'd better get one now, this year, because otherwise I'll be in big trouble next year.'

So I made a tape and I sent it to the Mean Fiddler, and they have an open-mike night, and I did a very short set. There were two other singers, it was one of those folk-ish evenings. Paul [Charles, her manager] was there, coming in for a cup of tea, from seeing Paul Brady, and he saw me and he liked me and then I had to leave to get the train to Basingstoke, and I didn't see him. Everyone was saying, 'Paul Brady's agent wants to talk to you', and I was saying, 'Oh, really' and I didn't even know what an agent was. I thought an agent was somebody really seedy, a cheeky chappie, really. But then I talked to him, and I started gigging, I was supporting lots of people and getting experience and then record companies started being vibed. They're very close in London, eventually a record company hears about you, everyone does, and they all start a bidding war. I just thought that's what happened, I really did. You're so innocent when you're young, in a way. You just accept things. And even the album was done so innocently and it was like, 'Oh, great, we're making an album', and the things just started happening. It was strange, but I thought that's what happened – OK, you make an album and it sells. Then you do all these interviews, then you do all these concerts. So it's only now that I think, 'that was strange', that's what's so odd, it happens so fast and it's only when you stop and you think, 'What have I been doing? I don't remember half the things I've done, I don't remember people, I don't remember places', but now I think I treasure things more, if I do anything or I go anywhere, I take more notice but I don't think I did [then]. There was no feeling of, 'Oh, that happened!'

I think part of that was about denial, it wasn't happening to me! I didn't read the press [coverage] and I still don't now really unless it's something that I think I'd enjoy but now I talk to friends and I say, 'wasn't that an odd time', it seems like an odd time and they always say, 'Well, it's inevitable that they'd say that about you', but they didn't recognise the person that was being written about; they'd say, 'That's not Tanita at all.' But then maybe it's not [journalists'] brief to understand you, it's just to put an idea of you into the public's mind, and if you're dark and if you've got black hair and you wear black clothes . . .

When I started, I really didn't have any idea, I could just do it. Fine, I can sing. I wasn't even aware that I have a low voice until people started telling me things like this. And then, at some point, I thought, 'This is real, why do I do this?' I had to think about that, otherwise I would have stopped. So I actually started becoming OK about performing in front of people. The biggest problem, I think, is accepting that people are coming to see you because I don't think when I started, I quite understood that. It was just bizarre. Now, I can think, 'Yes, I have this effect, hopefully, if I'm all that good, if I'm feeling this thing, then I can affect people', and I'm always surprised that I *can* do that. But, I think it's interesting how a woman performs, and how when you see men [perform] it's such a macho thing, not all men, but so much of it is bravado, and to me, that's the most boring experience I can have, is to see somebody doing that because that has nothing to do with music. Maybe it has something to do with glamour, something I don't really have much time for, but when you see somebody get on the stage, and they sing a song and you're taken away, that's real.

For two years I was touring, I loved it and I had a band that I really loved, and a crew that I loved, and I think, when I started, I didn't really have that. But the only thing about touring, it is a bit alienating because I toured with eleven men and *that* can be kind of alienating. It's like being in a gang which I quite like but then, it is a bunch of guys, although they're really not 'boysy', they're all really nice guys. I hate 'boysy' boys, I hate that kind of macho rock attitude. I was touring, recording, touring, recording, and then I stopped for about two years. I was writing still. I only stop writing because you need to stop to start again but that's very constant, that's very real. Even when everything else is going on around you, that's something that keeps you in touch with yourself. Writing is the real me, more than anything I do, apart from maybe singing. That's just a way of knowing myself.

The things I find hard I just think I should laugh at, like promotion. I don't dislike it but I'm quite passive in that way, I don't feel that I have anything to say, or I find I want to say, 'Why don't you listen to the record', and obviously that's the wrong attitude! It's like a little kid getting attention, and 'If I tell you this, I'll have more attention'. It's a very odd thing. In America, it seems that people have got it as scripts and they say, 'Oh, I was abused and I did drugs and I did this and that', and it's like they have a whole list. I don't understand it, but I watch it!

But I had that much in me so was very impatient to do it, though maybe that's self-defeating because people don't have the time to listen. But I had that in me, and I think after 'Eleven Kinds of Loneliness', I thought, 'What's it all about then', and I stopped, which is fair enough. And now I feel ready to start again. I needed to just meet people my own age, to hang out and see my friends and my family and to catch up. Also to travel. This is my ideal way of life, because I think I'm very lucky and I can travel and I can spend time here and there, and I'm writing so I'm feeling artistic in my life, but it's not some mad thing . . . often when you're touring, and doing promotion and all that stuff, it does feel that you're chasing some impossible dream, which isn't *your* dream. It's just so you can go into a newspaper shop and they say, 'I saw you on the telly last night, and I hadn't seen you on the telly for a long time, so what are you doing then?' And that's fair enough, but it's not that significant really. I just needed time because there is a very particular mentality which you're always exposed to which isn't necessarily one that I admire, and I just wanted to live my life and see my family, and meet other people whose lives weren't all about 'chart action'.

I wasn't aware of image until one of my friends said to me, 'Tanita, you have to be serious, because people don't like a jolly Tanita' and I didn't even understand. And I think only in the last two years has my innocence really gone, that I've suddenly thought 'I can just see through it', and it's not something I enjoy. I'm not cynical, but it's so banal; I can just see what people are trying to do. I think people are richer than that, they don't need to be [like that]. Especially in Los Angeles, unless you present something quite banal to somebody, it's unbelievable how they don't know how to talk to you. An interviewer doesn't know how to deal with somebody unless you're saying something . . . When I hear some people talk, sometimes I think, even if they're quite sophisticated, and quite serious artists, there's a sort of 'selling', like 'this is what I want you to know about me', I guess that's clever but it just doesn't seem very clever. It's difficult sometimes, because they don't even ask you the right questions. Sometimes I think, 'What have you heard on this song?' And so many interviews are done by men who reduce women's writing; all women's writing is just belittled, I think. As soon as they start, they say, 'women's writing is to do with the interior', as if that's a criticism. I don't know how you can write a song without it coming from inside, it's a bizarre concept, really. So, I have a big problem with that.

I was really happy about Nanci Griffith and Suzanne Vega . . . But what was offensive about the way people talked to you was that they weren't really listening – there was just 'Suzanne Vega, Tanita Tikaram, Tracy Chapman, you put them all together and there isn't any difference'. It was just a way of saying, 'I've got that sussed'. And you would just be infuriated when you were talking, because they [interviewers] weren't actually saying anything very interesting, and you would be put in the position where you'd have to be on the defensive, saying, 'Well, I'm not really like her actually'. I don't think I even mentioned when I started that I really loved Suzanne Vega's work, because I just didn't want this comparison.

First of all, I suppose, when they write about you, they have to write about something so, I guess if I was a guy they might write about . . . how I was like Leonard Cohen . . . I think it's a nice thing. I'm beginning to accept that there's something very nice about being a woman and about having that tradition of voices, because that's quite special really, and I've only begun to see that in a positive way. I think the problem with the media is that it's often very lazy and it's not really talking about things which are really interesting about the way women are or the way that women relate to each other . . . it's just lazy . . . it's not done with any passion, or any interest. But actually, I think there is something that I feel now, and I can accept that I feel that I might have my mother's voice. Or sometimes when I can't talk I think . . . maybe that's just because women haven't been allowed to talk for thousands of years, and now I have this voice, I feel quite self-conscious about it. You have to learn to use it. And so when there are more women about, allowed to use their voices, that's empowering, but it's just that you have to accept that the media, whatever it turns its head to, will make things simple or simplistic, and it won't be very sympathetic and that's not something that I can really change. Hopefully talking to someone like you, we can talk about things in a more interesting way.

It's bizarre: I've had people say, 'Why are you the same all the time?', and the next thing, they go 'Why do you try to be different all the time?' I think, 'I'm sorry!', it's a laugh though. What I find hard is that people don't listen, or people aren't allowed to listen to that kind of music, it doesn't have the immediate impact, as some pop music does. I think there are ways of talking about the music that belittles it, that it's obscure, that it's difficult and it isn't. People have a passion for it and they can care about it. I think sometimes people who write about music don't actually care very much about it, and I do, and I can see that, and I find that upsetting, that there can be such a closed view from people who are supposed to promote it. Even like the last Suzanne Vega album ['99.9 F'], I thought it was beautiful but when I first heard it, I thought, 'My God, what the hell's she doing?' and then I spent time with it and I think it's her best piece of work. If you just dismiss things, and there's so much product, probably that's the problem, then people are never going to find those gems, really. That's what I worry about sometimes. Sometimes I think people are not listening, they're not allowed to listen, they don't know how to listen to things, they're scared off by either language or different ways of using the language. And that's not very good, because it means that we're not allowing ourselves just to look at things in detail and that scares me slightly, because sometimes I turn on the telly and I think [of music programmes], 'What is this? I don't fit in there, I don't know how I ever did fit in'. Everybody listens to songs, people of all ages, that's what I get from when I do concerts, but I think there is a sort of idea that it's a small thing, that you have to have a special sort of knowledge, and that's wrong, because even if you don't understand the lyrics, and that's just one way of approaching it, like sitting down and understand a poem . . . There is often a feeling that there needs to be something else, it can't just be a song, it has to be a song with a girl in a short dress.

I really felt with 'Eleven Kinds of Loneliness', a lot of things came from my own feelings at the time about being a woman. I know that sounds strange but I don't think a male critic is going to *get* that and that's the problem. Like I don't get 'cars and girls in the desert' but that doesn't mean that they say 'that [music] is small', because I think it's very small but they would never talk about a man's work in this way, but they will with women. It's not even on the agenda, it's not even there; they don't understand. That's what I'm talking about, it's the language they use, there's so much in life and this is such a small way of looking at life. And that's what I resent – they don't have the authority to talk about these things. It's so difficult, you begin to talk to [them] and you think, 'I don't know what to say to you, I cannot talk to you, we're not even going to start on the same level. We're just talking about different planets here.' The hardest thing is that sometimes people aren't very warm, and I know that if somebody is warm towards me, I can talk to them forever, but if somebody isn't, I just want to hide. So, I don't think the warmest people are naturally interviewers, and that's strange to me, because I would have thought one of the most important things about talking to somebody is that you can be warm, and I'm often struck sometimes by this wall and I think, 'What are they thinking?' Maybe I just worry too much about other people and what they're thinking!

I love what I do, but eventually what happens is that you end up saying such a load of rubbish! It's like if you're at a dinner party, and somebody sits next to you and you think, 'What a nightmare, I'll have to move now', but you can't, you just sit there and you start saying the most banal things, and eventually you start saying, 'we used five musicians on this one', and you just cannot have a dialogue, that's the problem, you just end up saying things that you don't even believe, and you might as well be reading your biography. And I want to talk in a passionate way about what I do because it's important to me, but I guess I just have to turn off, but how many people honestly can just turn off? It's impossible, and it does hurt me because I don't like sitting in front of somebody, feeling like I come from outer space. That isn't why I do this. I think now that that is a part of my innocence gone. Maybe that's why, when I started, people just thought I was awkward and shy when really I was just bemused, in the same way that a kid will just look at an adult and know when they're telling the truth or not, and I felt very much like I had that sort of perception of things.

In singing, I think I'm the most honest I am. I don't think I'm very articulate when I'm talking to people, and I'm quite aware of that, and I'm quite self-conscious about the fact that when I'm talking to people I can't say what I want to say, and I think about it afterwards and think, 'God, why didn't I say this'. And only in the music, singing and performing, do I feel that I'm actually talking to someone and it's a very intimate thing, and that I'm actually allowing myself to be who I can be. There isn't anything more intimate than when I feel that I've connected and that I'm in some space, which is what music does really – it just puts you somewhere where no one can touch you, and that's probably why I do it. Because there's nothing that moves me in the same way.

————————————————■————————————————

I want to see people changing, and I want to see what they're feeling because that's what moves me, and I hope that people who spend time with the albums see changes. I think that with ['Eleven Kinds of Loneliness'] I changed an awful lot and I felt so strong when I did that, and I don't know if I could do that again. I was just very aware of what I wanted to do musically, and . . . even if it was just an illusion, I really thought that I was saying things differently, and I felt things differently, and I had grown up and there were things I had to say about myself and about my world. That was such a driving passion when I did the album that I was just buzzed by it. I don't think my record company liked it very much though, but some people I know love it, it's the album they love the most. I think some people were kind of offended that there were songs where I sang in different keys or things are raw. I like the idea that a woman can be quite aggressive in that way, not in a way that repeats that sort of rock-and-roll kind of aggression, which isn't aggression at all really, it's just posturing. But there are things inside you which are angry or hurt and that means different voices and different characters and different parts of yourself and some people cannot accept that in somebody. They find that quite threatening . . .

I think when you really yearn for something, and maybe you haven't experienced it, that's very poignant and . . . you arrive at some emotional truth somehow, because of your desire . . . you have felt everything, that's what I don't understand, you've felt it all and you've probably felt it ten times more because you haven't experienced it, and people forget that you've lived a thousand lives inside and that's where it all comes from. I can't say that, on this date, this happened to me and God, it was so sad, but I can say, 'I dreamt about all this and it was real to me'. I think that's where it came from. I had a friend who was going through a break-up, and he's listened to 'Eleven Kinds of Loneliness' and he came in every day and said 'This is me!', and I'm saying 'Yes, that's really good'. That's what's so special, that's how you should react to any piece of art, or anything creative, you should go up to someone and say, 'You know I saw that movie, and it just made sense to me'. How else is it going to be real to you?

Even my mother will come up to me and say, '"Elephant" is about me, isn't it, it's about my life'. And I'll say, 'Yes'. And it's great that you can do that and somebody will think that much of you, that you've touched somebody. Isn't that what people want to do anyway, they want to feel real? And you feel real when people have related to you in some way.

[People] write letters saying 'I know you'll never read this', and they tell you about their lives. I love that and I answer them. If people spend that much time listening to you, you should have the courtesy to reply. And it's interesting to know what moves somebody about what I do. I got a letter from Mongolia, which is kind of nice! And that's just bizarre, that your songs are in some part of the world which you've never been to. It makes you look at your work in a different way. Sometimes I go back and listen to the songs, and think, 'Yes, I can see that' . . . I always think songs have an infinite number of meanings.

I don't want to stand still and think about what I might have done because eventually you will improve, you will do different things. I think I'm quite single-minded and I think I know what's good, and I know *myself*. I like to see how people react to the voice and now I'm beginning to understand that people do react to my voice and that's the first thing. But really it has to be my own sense [of it] otherwise you'd go mad; people have so much baggage when they talk about you, that really, you can't really listen to it. I remember people coming up to me and saying, 'difficult second album', and I didn't know what they were talking about. And I think I didn't until now, it's like the difficult fifth album, not because it's difficult but because I can feel pressure for the album to perform commercially, which I've never felt before.

Ultimately, I don't care, because I *can't* care. I tried very hard to have a New Year's resolution to be very mature, and talk to everybody and have meetings and things because in some ways I felt I wasn't really communicating with my record company. But if I'm being honest, it's only now that I'm actually thinking 'the album has to do something commercially'. I've always said it's a bonus, it's a nice thing, but it isn't what it's all about. But you can't really have a meeting and say 'that isn't what it's all about'!

I like the idea of being a writer, though I think writing is becoming a bit like music, it's becoming incredibly commercial. If there was a Golden Age, where artists just . . . like Leonard Cohen, who doesn't really produce that much work when you think about it . . . I quite like the idea that it's a journey and every now and again, you tell people about this journey, through your music. That to me seems very sensible, instead of chasing something which is of no value, really no value at all. When I'm playing with my niece, she'll say 'And you're Number One!' and I think, even when you are Number One the only thing you worry about is that you're going to be Number One next week, and you don't worry about writing a great song, your concerns become alien to you, you end up worrying about achieving Number One . . . It's like a complete marketing thing, it's bizarre, it's like, 'OK, we've got to do this this week, and we've got to get Radio One on this, and we've got to get some TV [appearances] and we've got to advertise.' It's like something out of a movie . . . and it's not what I'm interested in. Then again, I also believe that a great song should be heard by a lot of people, in the way that The Beatles were, so I have a bit of a contradiction. It's the only indication you have that people are actually listening to your work, and it's all very well for me to sit here and say 'I'm just an artist and I do my stuff', but what's nice about having successful albums is that people hear it, no matter how they hear it, it's there.

I try to be disciplined but I can't. I think some of the greatest songs came out of Tin Pan Alley where the writers came in and sat down, and I'm fascinated by that, and by the great songs that came out of that manner of working, but I can't do that. I've only done that when I've written with other people, and then I think you get very generalised songs, which are fine, in a way they are a different kind of song, but I prefer for myself just to have something, some voice, or little obsession which comes out. I have to be inspired, and there are certain periods in the year when I'll be inspired for about six weeks, and then people can talk to me normally, and I'm back to normal. It's almost like there are periods when I have the Muse and other times when I'm just waiting for the Muse, and I get moody and difficult to live with. It's odd, sometimes it's almost as if someone is telling me about the future and I write songs and then suddenly all these things happen to me, or they're just things that I've been thinking about and they come out in songs. Sometimes I'm very shocked by how honest I think I've been but I don't think people pick up on that so it's different really, it changes, but I think they're little obsessions and then they come out.

Janis Ian

J anis Ian was born in New Jersey in 1951. She grew up in a creative, politically aware family which encouraged her writing. She had begun writing folk songs at age twelve, sending them to a music magazine, *Broadside*, which published one, 'Hair of Spun Gold'. She began performing her songs in folk clubs in New York. She met producer Shadow Morton, who encouraged her to record her composition 'Society's Child', the story of a doomed inter-racial teenage romance and parental hypocrisy. Atlantic Records paid for the recording session but refused to release the single, because of its controversial nature. More than twenty other record companies also turned it down.

Ian was finally signed by the Verve/Forecast label which released 'Society's Child' as a single; it provoked a storm of controversy and was banned by some radio stations. The conductor Leonard Bernstein championed Ian and featured her performing the song on his television show, 'Inside Pop – the Rock Revolution'. This led to widespread radio air-play and pushed the song into the US Top Twenty. Her debut album, 'Janis Ian', reached the US Top Forty and was nominated for a Grammy award for best folk album.

The following year, her album 'A Song for All the Seasons of Your Mind' was released and her hopes of performing at the Newport Folk Festival were dashed when the festival's organisers voted her too young – at sixteen – to perform. In 1968, she did appear at the festival after folk legend Pete Seeger sent her an apology for the decision. At the end of that year, 'The Secret Life of J. Eddy Fink' (Ian's given name) was released; followed by 'Who Really Cares' in 1969 and her debut for Capitol Records in 1970, 'Present Company'. Two years later, Roberta Flack had US Top Forty success with the Ian composition 'Jesse', which Ian herself recorded on the jazz-folk tinged album 'Stars' on Columbia Records in 1973.

In 1975, the album 'Between the Lines' featured what would become Ian's best known contemporary work, 'At Seventeen', a classic portrayal of adolescent isolation and insecurity. It was her first million-selling single, and the following year she was nominated for five Grammy awards. She was voted best female vocalist and the album and single won a total of three awards. In 1978, the album 'Janis Ian' failed to capitalise on this but the 1979 release, 'Night Rains', marked her first significant UK success with the single 'Fly Too High'. The song was written and recorded by Ian and producer Giorgio Moroder, for the Jodie Foster film, 'Foxes'.

Ian featured once again in the Grammy nominations when, in 1981, her duet with Mel Torme on her composition 'Silly Habits' was nominated in the best jazz vocal duet category. The same year saw her last studio release for a decade, 'Restless Eyes'. The next ten years were marked by long periods of disillusionment, despair and, finally, renewal: a violent marriage ended in divorce and she moved to Los Angeles to study drama and writing with Stella Adler, dance with Dora Kranning of the Paris Opera, and directing with Jose Quintero. In the mid-1980s she faced bankruptcy after discovering that the manager she had had since the beginning of her career had not paid her tax bills for years. To pay the mounting debts she sold all of her belongings except for her clothes and guitars and, in 1989, moved to Nashville, Tennessee, where she began to thrive, writing songs for others rather than recording her own. Her songs have been covered by artists as diverse as Nanci Griffith, Cher, Bette Midler, Stan Getz, Joan Baez, Ute Lemper, Chet Atkins, and Hugh Masekela.

Various compilation retrospectives of her work were released, but she returned to recording in 1992, with 'Days like These', for the soundtrack of the John Mellencamp film, *Falling from Grace.* Her first album in more than a decade was released on the Morgan Creek label in 1993. 'Breaking Silence' marked a personal and professional renewal, combining the lyrical love songs and social commentary of old: 'His Hands' described a violent marriage, 'Tattoo' chronicled the long-term suffering of a Holocaust survivor and 'Breaking Silence' was an account of the effects of child abuse. The album title was also widely interpreted as describing Ian's decision to publicly acknowledge that she was a lesbian. In the 1970s, she had spoken of her bi-sexuality, but by the early '90s, felt that the issues of AIDS and anti-homosexual bias called for a stronger public statement.

Janis Ian lives in Nashville.

It's a funny thing, depending on my moods, when I'm in a sour mood it seems to me that I have lived way too many lives for one human being; I'm forty-two, it's not exactly like I'm in my nineties! But when I look at someone who has eight kids by the time they are twenty-five, and I know someone like this, and works in a factory, I've had a really easy life, so I guess it all depends on your perspectives. Somebody read my cards once and the first thing they said was, 'You chose to re-do all those lifetimes at once?' It seems to me that as soon as I learn one big lesson and I get done learning it, I'm given about a year off and then this other huge thing happens. For a long time, I thought that maybe it was just that I courted drama, but it's not, because really just standing still, as my ex-husband used to say, one can make enemies standing still. And if I just stand still, things happen. I don't think that I could write the kind of songs that I write and not experience a lot of stuff. I think I've been real lucky in that I wasn't molested as a child, you know, stuff like that really bypassed me completely, so I have a pretty good foundation.

My mom used to say nothing could have stopped me and I think that's true. From the minute I picked up the guitar when I was about eleven, and wrote a song when I was about twelve or thirteen, that was all I wanted to do with my life. That was very clear. I've never quite understood people who don't know what they want to be when they grow up, because I have always known, I don't remember not knowing. So I knew when I was three that I wanted to be into music. I think it's a two-way street. On the one hand, nothing could have stopped me, I would have beaten down any door that I had to beat down. On the other hand, I guess most people do not have a song like 'Society's Child' as their beginning, and in that sense that was extraordinary.

Not everyone gets to open their career with that kind of statement; not everyone has the kind of family that I had, all of my family were very much activists in a non-hysterical way, and I was raised real strongly to believe that truth exists, justice exists, that the good guys *can* win. One must fight on the side of the angels, whatever the cost. I was raised with that as something that defined me as a human being, that separated me from the animals.

No one had ever told me growing up, that there was anything that I couldn't do because I was female. It wasn't in my family's vocabulary. My brother always washed dishes, I always had hunting knives, so in that sense, the fuss being made over things like wearing dresses made no sense to me, and in that sense it wasn't damaging because it never connected with me. But the amount of stupidity: whether you should have long or short hair, whether you should wear long earrings!

I was fourteen and a half when I wrote 'Society's Child'. If you talk to fourteen-year-olds and you get them to talk to you, they're having some pretty deep thoughts, that's a time of real questioning and coming of age, and learning about yourself. I think I was young and mature to be able to articulate those thoughts, but I don't think I was young to have them. That whole time period from about twelve to nineteen is just fraught with trauma. And so much of it is internal. All the other kids I knew were talking about the same things, it's just, I guess my gift is articulation. If I have one gift, it's that.

I had no idea what would happen. To me it was very cool

that I made a record and I heard it played on the radio. This was '66, the record business was still very small and fifty thousand records was a gold record; the stakes were much lower. No one expected that it would have that kind of impact on people. It's like 'At Seventeen', you don't expect to have that amount of impact. I don't find myself particularly brave; I find that I've spent my whole life doing things because they seemed like the right thing to do, and sometimes, when you are always doing the thing that seems right, it ends up being, in retrospect, a brave choice. I don't think you know when you are making the choice. Coming out with all the media, to me, was equal to a 'brave' choice, but it wasn't a choice. So I look back at 'Society's Child', I think that Shadow, the producer, just felt that it would make the best record. The record company released it and were very discouraged but got enough feedback from people in the industry who loved it, to keep re-releasing it, which was extraordinary. I can't imagine that happening now, to release a single three times over two years. It would get played here and there, and then banned here and there, and then they'd re-release it. I didn't realise at the time how hard it was, until I had a breakdown a couple of years later.

I was about seventeen and a half, eighteen, when I just had a major nervous breakdown. I was absolutely useless to anyone, most of all myself. I can't tell you what it is like to have that amount of hatred directed at you, it's the most bizarre thing. The only thing I can compare it to, is if you've ever had someone really really angry at you to the point where you thought 'my life is in danger', then you multiply that by thousands. That comes sort of close to that sense of being safe nowhere, of having nowhere to run, risking your life every time you walk out on the street. The amount of bomb threats we used to get, the amount of death threats we used to get, even nowadays those things are hard to cope with, then it was just nobody knew what to do. You know, nobody had bodyguards, no one had a clue about how to handle any of those things.

Couple that with the fact that because I was under-age, because I was female, there were a lot of things that I was not allowed to do, and it hit the point around the end of my third album, where they literally took the studio tapes away from me. The producer didn't show up, I was not allowed to continue the sessions, it kept costing me money anyway, and they wouldn't give me back my tapes, which really for me is always the bottom line, is the work you know. And, my parents got divorced shortly after 'Society's Child' was a hit.

Everything just happened at once. Then I left school which was great, but which was also weird, and I think that just outside of any of that, the kind of kid I was dictated that sooner or later I would have to fragment and get put back together. It's almost as though there was too much in there for anybody to hold. I needed to sort it out, and I had no idea at that age about how to even begin to sort it out. Now, I've had some real good therapy in my life, I've become very stable in my own head because I've become real clear of my priorities. But at that age, you can't be clear on anything, and your hormones are just raging. Now I separate out the writer in me, the performer in me, and the lover in me. I don't bring them to each other all the time. There's not all this constant cross-talk. Then, I had no separation from anything, you know, everything was just one big ball. And it was terrifying.

I suddenly realised that people were really listening to me, people were hanging on to the words and they were living their lives by what I said. And given how responsibly I was raised, the responsibility of that was just daunting. I didn't feel like I had any right to their ears. I didn't feel like I was a writer. I think it is just so powerful, that there's a responsibility when you say something and you have an audience. My responsibility as a songwriter, then my responsibilities as a performer to the audience, and in that sense, I didn't feel that I was a good enough writer that people should be listening to me. And I wasn't.

In terms of the controversy, I think it left a lot of scars just because the concept that someone can hate you for what you sing was so novel to me. I was totally unprepared for the kind of viciousness that I encountered. Then again, if I look back now that kind of viciousness was really, and is really, on its way out.

It's not something that is socially acceptable. Then, there were areas of the country, entire states, where we didn't play – Alabama, Mississippi – because of the level of hate mail that we got. Things have changed a lot and it's nice to think that maybe ['Society's Child'] was a small part of the change.

It is really only in the last five or six years that I have had the distance to look on it and say, 'that was really hard'. But I don't think that it was any harder on me than it would have been on anyone else. There are two separate issues: there's the fame and there's the controversial aspect. In terms of the fame I don't think anyone is prepared to deal with it. It is never what you think it is going to be. The amount of minor back-biting is always new, the idea that everything you do is going to affect your future. That there is no privacy, for someone like me who was just beginning as an artist, to have to work out all of their art in a goldfish bowl.

Most artists have a formative period in their teens and their twenties. I never had the formative period. It was all right out there so those things were really hard, the schedule was hard, the most distinct part of it to me was just the aloneness. I didn't have a band, I didn't really have anyone around me. I wish that someone like me had come to me and said, as I have done with a couple of younger performers, 'Here's the deal, and here's what will happen if this happens, and here's what won't happen if this doesn't happen!'

A female artist, not a female singer, but a female artist, didn't have any role models then, except in jazz. I didn't know any other females who were writing their own material and only a handful who were writing at all. Buffy Sainte Marie wrote a couple of songs on her record. That was it. Nina Simone was about the only female singer-songwriter I knew of who could in any way, shape or form be a role model. There wasn't anybody out there for me to talk to. For me to strut in with a guitar and say, 'I'm the girl and I play a guitar', was unheard of. For me to arrange, to lead a band, to be in on the sessions, was unheard of. It just wasn't done. I had no idea that I was breaking ground, and it's only in the last five or six years, as people like the Indigo Girls have come and thanked me, that I realise that I did break ground. It wasn't a decision, it wasn't a choice, it was just, 'Well, of course, I'm telling the band what to play, I wrote the songs!'

I had this real interesting lunch with Donny Osmond once, and we were talking about the role models for child stars. I mean there were the Gatlin brothers in country music and Brenda Lee in bop, there was Stevie Wonder, me and Donny. That was it, and of them, Stevie and I were the only ones writing our own material, and I was the only girl writing raw material. So it was really uncharted.

———————————————— ■ ————————————————

Record contracts become harder to get, every year. When I was a kid there were twenty-two companies that turned down 'Society's Child' and there were twenty-two major record companies in the United States. There are now five. Everything is an arm of one of those companies, and in that sense you are dealing now with the companies that are owned by the makers of hardware, who are only interested in manufacturing software. When you get into selling software it's very visual. If you cannot be manufactured visually now, I don't think you can have a career. And that is really criminal, because if you look at the seminal influences on blues, on music in America, on rock and roll, which you could argue is an indigenous American form, or jazz, these were not good-looking women. If you take Bessie Smith or Billie Holiday, Nina Simone, Ella Fitzgerald, these were not good-looking women at all. They are not the standard pretty. I find Nina beautiful but that's because she's striking, not because she's pretty. With the men, you can't say Miles Davis was handsome – and John Lennon, Bob Dylan, really! So in that sense it's getting worse and worse, as there's more media.

I think it's very difficult now, especially if you're female, because so much is expected of you. You should be like Tori Amos and be very sexual, and be very thin, and very pretty and kind of an ethereal waif like Suzanne Vega, and still have the strength to be an artist. It is very difficult to be an artist. For someone like me I think it is even worse because I fall into that 'women over forty' category now, where I am Janis Ian so I can sell X units just by being, but I am also a female over forty. I'm not going to go out and do *anything*. I'm not going to go on tour all year, and I'm not as saleable because I'm not new. In that respect it gets harder and harder. And worth less and less to me, I think.

———————————————◼———————————————

I wanted to be the first pop kind of mainstream female to come out [as a lesbian], because I wanted to set a precedent. But k d lang beat us by three months! I knew in '89, when I spoke to my business manager about looking for a record contract, that I had to come out and come out very publicly, and I was ready to do it in '89 but we didn't get a contract. I realised how damaging it was for me not to come out, not for me, but how much it would mean if I did come out that loudly and publicly, because I had always been in the school of 'well, it's my private life'. And what I realised was that until enough people like me come out loudly, it will have to be our private lives, we'll have no choice.

I realised how much of it was a civil rights issue, what a bad example it was for kids, for someone like me to be closeted. What it said to some fourteen-year-old, that they were sitting right around going, 'Janis Ian is probably gay', as opposed to 'well, she's gay, she says so'. The example that Pat and I could set of a stable homosexual couple, who look pretty innocuously normal and who, at my end, was already in people's living-rooms. The fact that I was in a stable relationship, the fact that I had a step-daughter, became a factor. I didn't want anyone to be able to 'out' me, I didn't want anyone to think that I was ashamed in any way of my gender preference, or of my partner, because what does that say about your partner? Once we decided that, I told my parents, because I wanted them to be prepared for any fall-out, and my brother and his wife, and I discussed it with the people in [Gay and Lesbian Task Force]. Urvashi Vaid was president then, and she felt strongly that I should wait until the album came out, to do the most good. When the album came out, one of the things we did as part of the regular press package was just list it as one of the topics they might find of interest, and everybody just jumped on to it. It was the year of lesbian chic, all of a sudden I was in, hip, for the first time!

I know here and there which record companies turned me down because they did not want another lesbian on their label; to quote one of them: 'We've got enough lesbians already!' The quota is filled! By and large it has been really positive. What has been very gratifying to me is that I had worried a little bit that people who are ignorant very often do not want their kids around, or role-modelling, gay people. They don't realise how many other kids already role-model gay people. People who think they've never met one, you know, and it's been very gratifying to me that, if anything, the requests for me to do things with children have stepped up. That makes me feel good, that makes me have some hope that the world is not such a strange place.

I haven't gone out and gone on all the TV shows, presenting myself as 'lesbian of the month'. I talk about it because I think it is healthy to talk about it to the press, and it's good for kids to read. Everybody is now saying why didn't you write 'At Seventeen' for gay people? I don't have *that* much control over what I write! They're meaning a song that will really embody all the things gay people go through; it's valid and I'd love to be able to write it. But I didn't sit down to write 'At Seventeen', I was really writing a song about my teenage years. Some things just come when they come.

No one knows what it feels like to come out of that closet until they're out of it. You can't describe the joy, you can't describe what it is like to no longer live in the shadows. You also can't tell anybody that it will be safe. From the severely 'closeted' performers that I know – we're talking about people who are not just closeted with the press, but take boyfriends or girlfriends to industry functions, and sometimes even marry – I think it makes you crazy. They try to be in two places at once, and you can't. It's living in a state of total denial.

The people I know who are closeted very often are not performers but are people who would lose their jobs, who might lose their families, who would lose their children. In the state of Tennessee if you are a homosexual parent, it doesn't matter if the other parent is a drug addict or a felon, you do not get custody. So in that sense it's more than a risk. For some people it's their lives. I don't think you can dictate someone's fate to them.

My whole bisexual thing was printed in the mid-'70s, but the press have always been good to me. I think if I had said that at the height of 'At Seventeen', I would have had no career. 'At Seventeen' would not have been played. The times didn't allow it. I would like to believe that quality outs, but it doesn't always, and that's the sad truth of it. I will never know how much of any lack of sales or lack of air-play in any specific country comes from that. In Japan there is not even a word for 'lesbian', there's no concept of it. They will tell you straight-faced, particularly males, that there are no female homosexuals there. What does that do to my career there? So, in that sense I took a very real risk and I do think there has been some fall-out.

When I do something like Howard Stern's [radio] show, that I have taken an extraordinary amount of shit for doing, I'm thinking of his audience of 15- to 25-year-old, white red-neck males, buying my record, and carrying away some of those ideas. I think about those kids seeing an open lesbian interacting with a by and large straight audience. Not proselytising, not over-politicising it, just stating things, they have a good time and they go away and maybe the next time somebody wants to stomp a faggot they remember that.

When I sing 'His Hands', you can see in the audience who is uncomfortable and who's not. Maybe that makes for a change. Maybe some kid is listening to 'Breaking Silence' in their bedroom at night in secret, knowing that there is someone out there who says, 'this is wrong'. And because, when you are being molested as a kid, so much of it is that you don't feel like anyone will stand up for you. We get all that mail in the fan-club about that kind of stuff, so I have to figure that it's having some effect.

———————————————— ■ ————————————————

One of the things that happened to me after that period of silence from when I was about eighteen to twenty-one was that I wrote 'Jesse', I wrote 'Stars', and I decided that I *was* a writer. I made one of those logarithmic leaps that you make as an artist, that now looking back I don't understand why I haven't made a million of them!

I didn't have any credibility from when I was twenty or twenty-one and we started looking for a record contract. I was entering into the arena of 'has-been', 'used-up', 'child prodigy'. It didn't matter what I wrote, people saw it through that filter. When I started going on the road again in '72, we used to have tooth and nail fights over not having me billed as 'Society's Child'. And I didn't even sing the song until five or six years ago. There is a point where people think you are being silent, and what you are actually doing is trying to get a gig, and nobody will give you the gig. And that happens to me a lot. When I stopped in '82, I stopped so that I could take two years and write; when I came back in '84 it was a whole other business, and since I had walked away from my Sony contract, I had to start all over again.

I thought, 'Well OK, I can't get a contract, I'm going to say I'm just a writer for the next two or three years.' And that's what I did. I signed a publishing deal in '86, and turned my back on recording for three years. And it was interesting because other performers [began recording] my songs because they weren't worried any more that I would do them, and usurp them.

Every time I hear something I'd like to record, I end up writing something that I like better. I have a pretty limited vocal range. It's about an octave and a half, two if I really push it. It's not a great instrument, just speaking technically. If you listen to 'Society's Child', and you listen to that 'At Seventeen' period, I worked very hard to make my voice sound like a voice that I would enjoy. I spent hours interning in various studios so I could use the equipment; every night they would let me go in with an assistant engineer and work and just learn to make my voice sound on tape like I heard it in my head. I was born with good pitch and good phrasing, but it's a quiet voice, it doesn't carry very well, so there's a limit on what songs I can sing without appearing ridiculous.

I love singing 'At Seventeen', I love singing 'Jesse'. Part of retaining creative control, which is a constant battle, is that I know better than anyone at this point that my songs may follow me in twenty years. Chances are unlikely now, I mean I'm forty-two, but even five years from now, I don't want to be put in a position where I won't sing a song that the audience wants to hear. We've put 'Society's Child' back in [the live show], because the bass player kept saying that people were coming up after the show and asking for it. How many times can people ask for something and you keep turning your back? Another type of artist might say, 'screw you, it doesn't matter', but I really feel that people who come to my shows have stayed loyal for long enough that they deserve something back.

——————————————■——————————————

The kind of writing that I do for my records is real truthful, and I think there's an authority that you gain from that truthfulness, that makes something like 'At Seventeen' work. It becomes problematic with something like 'Breaking Silence' where I kept trying to write about it in the first-person, and I just didn't feel that I had the authority, having not been molested. No matter how much I said 'I can imagine that or I have been in similar situations', I really can't imagine what it's like to be suicidal at the age of five. I have no frame of reference for that, or for bed never to be a safe place. I tried for about six years until I finally said, 'I can't do it' and put it into the observer, which I think worked much better. Something like 'His Hands', my ex-husband hit me, I know about that and so I can speak with some authority. I think it's rare that I've cut something that is first-person that I haven't felt, but I write a lot of things first-person that I wouldn't record because I don't have the authority.

If another artist comes to me and asks me to write something that they feel is about their life, but they are not writers, then I take on their authority and that's a different thing as well. It's a cool thing to me, because it is really someone saying, 'I trust you with my life'. Part of the luck of the draw in being an artist is that once in a while you hit the Zeitgeist, and you just hit it right on the head, your timing is perfect. Look at Prince, perfect timing. Dylan, if he'd been ten years earlier, would have had no career; The Beatles also. Your talent lies in your choices and I think that's probably the truest thing about talent, because you choose what you write, you choose what to present, and your real talent, your real gift, is in making the right choice.

———————————————— ◼ ————————————————

As a male [musician] you are supposed to somehow have mythically appeared! It's like the Dylan thing: 'No, no, I never read Rimbaud!' It's funny for me because I am always about ten years younger than my contemporaries and it's an odd place to be right now, because there is a school acknowledging that I influence them. I think it's very cool that they acknowledge it at all. I have heard that from Melissa [Etheridge] and the Indigos. That's an amazing thing to have happen. It's a respect to your past. It's like me acknowledging Baez or Nina or Billie Holiday. You look on a bunch of people a generation after you and go, 'Oh I see myself in their writing, I hear myself in their singing'. And yet it's odd because I don't feel that old. When I look at my contemporaries, people like Baez or Dylan, and they're ten, fifteen years older and I've always kind of fallen in that weird middle slot.

———————————————— ◼ ————————————————

If the '80s were anything for me, it was a loss of innocence. I learned that people can be bad even when they seem good, and that you really can't trust anyone past a certain point, because at the end of the day you are alone. That's a very harsh lesson. I think most people learn it a lot younger than I did, but it was obviously needed. It leaves me in a marriage with Pat, where I know that if she leaves, I won't die; it leaves me with a business manager that I can audit; it leaves me more in charge of my own life, for better or for worse.

With the continuing financial catastrophe, for the second time in my life, I was shattered. This person, who is dead now, had been my accountant since I was fifteen. If you want to talk about an ultimate betrayal, here's someone you've trusted with your money, your life, your family, your will, your executorship, for twenty years, and suddenly they turn out to have been stealing from you for a large part of that, and there's nothing you can do to get back that kind of trust.

There has got to be a point where you trust people, but there have also got to be safeguards. Between that betrayal, and I think any marriage, no matter how bad it gets to be, when it's over, it's the loss of a dream. You know, it's a death. If I can't look at it philosophically, I will go under. No human being can cope with this amount of angst, and not go under, unless you develop some kind of perspective.

Book List

The following books were particularly helpful in the preparation of this book:

Joachim E. Berendt, *The Jazz Book* (Paladin, 1984).

Donald Clarke (ed.), *The Penguin Encyclopedia of Popular Music* (Penguin, 1989).

Gillian G. Gaar, *She's a Rebel: The History of Women in Rock and Roll* (Seal Press, 1992). This book deserves special praise – it is a superb, meticulously researched work which goes a long way to counter the effects of decades of neglect in standard rock histories. The preface is written by Yoko Ono.

Evelyn Glennie, *Good Vibrations: My Autobiography* (Hutchinson, 1990).

Dafydd Rees and Luke Crampton, *The Guinness Book of Rock Stars*, third edition (Guinness Publishing Ltd, 1994).

Suzanne Vega, *Bullet in Flight: Songs* (Omnibus Press, 1990).

Quotes (page ix) from *Like a Fish Needs a Bicycle: And Over 3000 Quotations By and About Women* ed. Anne Stibbs (Bloomsbury, 1992).

Other Virago books of interest

NEVER MIND THE BOLLOCKS
Women Rewrite Rock

By Amy Raphael
Foreword by Deborah Harry

'The voices here, whether they belong to Courtney Love, Björk, or Kim Gordon, are as diverse and difficult, as weird and wonderful as they are on stage' – *Suzanne Moore*

Top music journalist Amy Raphael takes us on a wild journey which takes the cock out of rock and explains how this new wave of women artists have been a long time coming, but now they are here, the face of modern music will never be quite the same again. With a major interview with Courtney Love, this book lets artists talk for themselves about their work.

Musicians include *Sonya Aurora-Madan and Debbie Smith (Echobelly)* • *Gina Birch (The Raincoats)* • *Tanya Donelly (Belly)* • *Ellyot Dragon* • *Kristen Hersh* • *Pam Hogg (Doll)* • *Huggy Bear* • *Liz Phair*

THE WOMEN'S COMPANION TO INTERNATIONAL FILM

Edited by Annette Kuhn with Susannah Radstone

Who was the only major woman director in Hollywood's heyday? Where, in cinema, does Kung Fu meet women's revenge? Find out the answers to such questions and many more in this pioneer reference book. Comprehensive in its coverage of the cinema perspective, and international in scope, this guide provides information about the women – and significant men – who have contributed to the cinemas of the world from the stars through the directors and producers to the gossip columnists and critics. It covers the history of film-making from the avant-garde to Hollywood making an invaluable addition to film, media and cultural studies, as well as being a pleasurable companion for cinema-goers worldwide.